The Saint and the Pig

A dream and how
St. Antonius is involved

LIVING HUMAN HERITAGE PUBLICATIONS, ZURICH

Studies from the

RESEARCH- AND TRAINING CENTRE
FOR DEPTH PSYCHOLOGY
ACCORDING TO C.G. JUNG AND MARIE-LOUISE VON FRANZ

THE SAINT AND THE PIG

A dream and how St. Antonius is involved

A psychological contribution

Regina Abt-Baechi

With a preface by M.-L. von Franz

Second extended edition

LIVING HUMAN HERITAGE PUBLICATIONS, ZURICH
2015

Frontispiece
Antonius der Einsiedler (Antonius the Hermit), 1430 AD. Ferdinand Eichler

Living Human Heritage Publications
Münsterhof 16, 8001 Zürich, Switzerland

info@livinghumanheritage.org
www.livinghumanheritage.org

ISBN-13 978-3-9524468-2-9

Layout: Merve Çakıroğlu and Theodor Abt

Print:
Mas Matbaacılık A.Ş.
Hamidiye Mahallesi Soğuksu Caddesi
No:3 34408 Kağıthane, İstanbul / Türkiye
T. +90 212 294 10 00 (pbx) F. +90 212 294 90 80
info@masmat.com.tr

Contents

Introduction

Many years have passed since I first worked on this topic and published my initial conclusions. With the passage of time, I came to realise that there was more to it than first met the eye and that further intensive work was required on the saint with the pig. This book is an updated and extended version of the original, based on my continuing study of Jungian thought and on my experience as an analytical psychologist.

I would like to thank my husband, Theodor Abt, for his commitment to this book and especially for his conscientious work with the editing and layout. My thanks also go to Sabine Mayer-Patzel for her diligence with regard to preparing the index, the proofreading and her friendly cooperation in so many different ways. Once again David Roscoe, with his love of language and his interest in Jungian psychology, came up with a translation that was up to his usual standard. I would also like to thank Alison Brown for her invaluable support and involvement in this project.

My greatest thanks go to Marie-Louise von Franz for her patience in accompanying me as I embarked on the task of seeking the fundamental meaning of my own dream. It not only led to this book being written, but also provided me with access to the collective meaning of archetypal dreams and a completely new approach to the problems of our time.

Oetwil am See, May 2015 Regina Abt-Baechi

Preface

In almost all cultures, outstanding personalities who have accomplished more than others in the fields of religion and therapy are venerated after their death, examples being the Buddhist Bodisattvas, the sheikhs in Islam, the shamans of the circumpolar cultures, certain 'big' medicine men in Africa and, last but by no means least, the saints of the Catholic Christian faith. With all of these personalities there is evidence that they have undergone the essential stages of what C. G. Jung referred to as the individuation process: A confrontation with the forces of destruction, disease and evil; the integrating of components of the opposite sex (which then often occur as attributes or pet animals) and the acquisition of "divine energies", which often virtually raise those who possess them nearly to the level of divine beings. In contrast to mere mortals, who remain only alive in the ancestor worship of the family, or a small circle at most, these great personalities become, so to speak, the living archetypal notion of whole nations.

Saint Antonius Eremita is a figure who exhibits these traits to a marked degree, and his appearance in a dream of the author reveals very clearly how such an archetypal image can spontaneously come alive, even in someone who does not profess the faith of the Catholic Church. In this dream, the cross he wears plays a particularly crucial role. This is apparently no coincidence, because the Christian mana personality shares the fate of the founder of the religion, and the symbol of the cross is at the very core of Christianity. As C.G. Jung sought to prove in his book *Aion*, the fate of Christ and his teachings is marked by an extreme polarisation of psychic opposites. The symbol of the self, the archetype of psychological totality, is split into a light and a dark side, personified in Christ and Antichrist or visible in the separation of the Kingdom of Heaven and the world of damnation. The cross symbolises the clash, the conflict, between these opposites, but also the assumption that they may possibly be reunited. The legendary characteristics of the Antonius image, established by popular belief, place more emphasis on the reconciling of the opposites than on the way they clash, thus paving the way for a development which seeks above all to manifest itself in the unconscious psyche of modern man. This is why these ancient legends seem to have retained an amazing topicality, which we appreciate more fully as a result of the author's interpretation. Her perceptive observations speak for themselves without the need for any further comment from me.

Küsnacht, August 6, 1983 Marie-Louise von Franz

Fig. 1: Antonius the Hermit. Statue of the Niederrotweiler Altar, at 1530.

1. My personal Situation

St. Antonius the hermit, commonly referred to as «Seu Antoni» or «Säuli-Toni», first came to my attention many years ago. It was a Monday, January 17th, and the farmers, dressed in their Sunday best, were making their way to church. It made a deep impression on me and I discovered that St. Antonius was seen here above all as the patron saint of cattle, pigs and domestic animals in general. This immediately struck a chord with me, but I only met him again much later on, during a period of great distress; it was in a dream, one which forms the basis of this work. Here is the first part of the dream:

We are in the church in the village where I grew up. The church has been completely modernised, as has the carillon. The bells are ringing out, but the sound is totally chaotic. It saddens me when I think back to the harmony and rhythm of the old bells. There is also disorder and chaos inside the church itself. The chairs are set out fairly tidily in a circle, but there is no altar in the middle; instead there are two of them just pushed to one side. The people are talking among themselves, just chattering about any old thing. I feel awful and see that my husband has already left and I do the same. This results that many of them stop talking and walk away.

The second part of the dream has been shortened:

In the home of M.-L. von Franz. It is a bit chaotic, but cosy and warm. I think that this a place for creative work. There are animals, too. We are cooking together in a cheerful atmosphere. There is a large picture of St. Antonius (like an icon) hanging on the wall. Above it, there is a large cross. M.-L. von Franz says that whenever the temperature changes (because of the sun?), the cross will drop into his arm or his hand. It also happens suddenly, and at first drops too far down [....].

The first part of the dream seems to depict a somewhat confused and forlorn attitude within a church lacking in order, harmony and reverence. Yet the memory of the bells that used to ring out so beautifully in the church before it was modernised, indicates that there was a time when the world was in order and religion had its rightful place. Maybe my Christian world was still intact when I was a child and, in my prayers, used to ask God to take all poor and tormented animals into His care. With great enthusiasm, I read the biography of St. Francis of Assisi. Whenever I could, I skipped Church instruction classes. Instead I would roam the woods with my dog at every opportunity; it was there, amidst the mysterious, magical, much loved world of Nature, that I believed I could find proof of the existence of a loving God. Around the time of my confirmation there was a profound and dramatic experience of death within my family. It was then that I seriously began to give thought to the question of who this God was to whom I would have liked to turn in my hour of need. The ensuing disappointment with the shallowness of what the minister and the church had to say on the subject created a great emptiness inside me. My enthusiastic childlike devoutness had faded away into nothingness, a lukewarm everyday rationality. What remained was a secret need to be deeply moved, a sort of devotion or dedication to sorrow, joy, gratitude or any vibrant, immediate feeling. It was a period of loss of inner orientation, one which lasted for some years. Then came the encounter with the psychology of C.G. Jung, which opened up a whole new psychological dimension for me. In the work with dreams that this led to, I was deeply affected by the miracle of the meaning that they contained, and slowly but surely there formed within me a feeling about the existence of something unimaginable, a completely personal experience of something that was somehow meaningfully at work beneath the surface of things.

In the second part of the dream, Antonius arrives on the scene. What was immediately striking about him was that his cross was only able to move down when there was a change in the temperature, i.e. a warming up.

For me, the change in temperature had something to do with feeling or feeling judgement, which apparently could bring about a change in my views. In the dream, the sun seems to be responsible for this rise in temperature. As it rises, the sun brings an end to the night and enables us to see the things of the day world. This is why, since time immemorial, it has been a symbol for consciousness and discerning understanding. So probably the dream image about a process of becoming conscious in relation to the picture of St. Antonius. I was surprised and wondered what this Catholic saint was doing in my dream since I had been raised as a Protestant and had later distanced myself from all conventional church beliefs.

At the time of the dream I had just become a mother with a new baby, caught up in the conflict between inner needs and external demands. Nothing seemed more impossible than embarking on an academic project, for that meant being able to tear myself away from the hectic pace of everyday activities and the demands of external life so as to be able to find peace and quiet for such work. Visiting libraries, tracking down books, was virtually impossible from the organisational point of view. It was a cross I had to bear! There was no Internet at that time. This field of tension was part and parcel of the whole project on the figure of St. Antonius, and I never knew where it would lead me, or indeed if it would lead me anywhere at all. It is thanks to the patient and constant support of Marie-Louise von Franz that this work actually came into being. She set me off on a path that was to change the course of my life.

In what follows next, I will deal first with the life of the saint and with the legends surrounding him, and then go into the significance of his attributes. My aim with this work was to arrive at a deeper understanding of the above dream, but it was only at the end that a meaningful interpretation began to take shape. My approach was based on the hypothesis put forward by C.G. Jung that there is a collective unconscious which represents, as it were, the reservoir and basis of general human ideas and concepts, out of which there emerges all culture and development of consciousness. If I had not had access to this groundbreaking hypothesis, I would have been at a complete loss with my dream. As it was, I still had to immerse myself in the work of C.G. Jung to find the tools which I had learnt might be of use to me. When I began to work, it simply did not occur to me to question what it might mean to a reader who had no interest in either psychological literature or, for religious reasons, in a Catholic saint. But M.-L. von Franz swiftly dispossessed me of any attempt to view my own dream as too personal and of little general importance.

Initially I could see very few connections with my own life, so I plunged into the broad sphere of general human and archetypal concepts which seemed to be connected with this figure, and immediately felt hopelessly lost. Wherever I looked in sagas, legends, fairytales, popular thinking and customs, there were lots of links in meaning and many common features to be seen. As all this material had its roots in the same unconscious human psyche from which the picture of the saint originated, everything suddenly seemed to mean everything and to lead everywhere. I soon had to accept that any attempt to create order in this jumble was a task that could not be accomplished with the ordering and regulating consciousness alone. I could not exclude myself, with my own personal relativism and hence with my feelings. That, in fact, had to be my starting point. Antonius was clearly first and foremost addressing me. However he had also something to say to countless generations of people in the past and he still speaks many people today. In other words: the picture of this saint as people imagined him, as they visualised him artistically, without really knowing why they did it the way they did, actually contains statements about the human soul that are valid generally but can only be fully understood through the medium of the individual life in a specific time and setting. The view into this dimension of the general human or the archetypal background was a crucial experience for me. It is what made me conscious of the anchoring of every culture and every individual in the unconscious psyche; it was really a breathtaking experience, which basically turned every rational world view upside down. But I had to establish the connection of the unconscious world of the archetypes to modern day-to-day reality. This was necessary for an understanding of the figure of Antonius but also partly entailed a element of painful limitation and restriction. It forced me to select individual elements from the wealth of material at my disposal and connect them to life and how I was affected personally.

The saint and the pig; an unusual combination – or so it appeared to me initially. As a livestock healer and special patron saint of pigs, Antonius, seems to have a friendly connection to the pig. This is actually not at all a Christian characteristic, for according to Christian thinking, Antonius should be hostile to the pig, which in modern terms is the embodiment of dirt and sin. Already at this stage we see a first striking contradiction in the figure of the saint, something that will preoccupy us throughout the whole of this work.

The basis for the following observations was provided by the pictorial representations of St. Antonius as well as by the attributes that appear most frequently in literary descriptions which, in addition to the pig, above all include fire, the bell, the cross and the book. The last-mentioned marks Antonius as the founder of the Antonius Order, which came into being in the Middle Ages but will not be discussed in detail here. At first glance, these attributes have an obvious meaning. The pig is generally regarded as the embodiment of the demons that tormented Antonius. The bell belonged to the Antonite monks, who were pig-breeders, and heralded their arrival in this way. The cross was regarded as the symbol for warding off demons and suchlike. However, we regard these attributes not just as signs of something familiar but as symbols which are to be viewed from all angles and then interpreted. Genuine symbols are never thought up consciously; they come into being from the background of the unconscious psyche, and according to C.G. Jung, they are the best possible expression of something unknown that cannot be expressed in any other way. Through this symbolic method of observation, the Antonius figure, as it has come down to us, has gained in depth and significance. As he is a Christian saint figure, he also has to be viewed against the background of Christianity and its historical development. From hermit and desert healer of the 3rd century to Patron of the Sick in the Middle Ages, the figure of Antonius underwent many changes along the way. With the passage of time, his symbolism seems to be increasingly tending towards extending and compensating certain one-sided features of the conscious Christian attitude. Also important are the legends, which tell of the encounters Antonius had with the Devil and challenges he faced.

Fig. 2: The Egyptian desert near the cave of Antonius.

2. Antonius the Hermit: his Life

There is a detailed description of the life of St. Antonius, the *Vita Antonii*, written by the Church father, Athanasius of Alexandria, who knew the Saint personally and had often visited him in the desert.[1] Furthermore, a number of letters from Antonius have been preserved although the authenticity of most of them has been questioned.[2] Historians regard the *Historia Lausiaca des Palladius*[3] and the *Vita S. Pauli des Hieronimus*[4] as the two *most genuine sources of information about the life of the saint.*

Antonius was born of quite wealthy Christian parents in Middle Egypt around the year 250. When he had just reached adulthood, his parents died. Shortly afterwards he gave up all his possessions, making a gift of his fields to neighbours and people of his village. His money he gave to the needy, not without first ensuring the future of his younger sister, for whom he found accommodation with pious women. He had thus deprived himself of the prospect of wealth and family happiness, but was now free to lead a spiritual life, which had probably long been his wish. To begin with, he stayed in the vicinity of his village, where he initially kept company with an old hermit, who initiated him into the basic principles of asceticism. Antonius then moved around, meeting various ascetics so that he could learn from them. It was at this stage that he first experienced doubts, fears about the future and resistance to a life of privation, his physical needs, and so he had to withstand his first struggles with the demons. Occasionally he worked to earn his living, but as he was popular people were often happy to do him favours.

1 Athanasius, Vita Antonii (VA)

2 The only letter definitely accepted as authentic is the one that Antonius wrote to a certain Abbot Theodor. Cf *Saint Antoine, Lettres*, Abbaye de Bellefontaine 176, p.10, p.111.

3 D.C.Butler, *The Lausiac History of Palladius*.

4 Detailed sources in: Aurenhammer, *Lexikon d. christl. Ikonographie*, p.15

Fig. 3: The entrance to the cave of Antonius.

After this period, Antonius decided to adopt an even more radical approach to cutting himself off from the outside world. He found himself an empty rock tomb, probably a cave on a mountain slope near the Nile, and that is where he lived, only occasionally having food brought to him. This tomb or cave was also the scene of his worst temptations from the Devil and struggles with demons. It is not clear how long this period of seclusion lasted. It might have been two, or it might have been twenty years. Antonius' next move led him even deeper into the desert to an even more isolated site for his life as a hermit. He found a level spot at the foot of a high mountain, where there was a spring and some date-palms. Here he made himself at home and began to grow corn and vegetables on a small piece of land so that he could provide for himself and not be dependent on passing caravans, which for a long time had brought him bread.[5]

Antonius was thus not one of those desert hermits who punished themselves with the most extreme forms of deprivation such as wearing heavy chains, starving to the very limit of survival, or living on top of a pillar, totally dependent on the mercy of others. Antonius' more modest approach to the hermit's life can be seen in the following short stories from the *Vita Antonii* by Athanasius.

A legend tells how boredom once overcame him in the desert. Then he said: «Lord, I would like to be blessed, but my thoughts won't let me.» So he got up and went out. And he saw someone sitting and working, then standing up and praying. It was an angel, who spoke to him and said: «Do likewise and you will be saved.»[6]

Ora et labora – pray and work – or spirit and earth: for Antonius, this created inner equilibrium.

The following story provides an apt illustration:

An archer once became annoyed because Antonius was making merry alongside the other brothers. So Antonius told him to keep tightening

5 Compare the concise and good summary of L.v. Hertling on the life of Antonius (in German): *Antonius der Einsiedler.*

6 *Die Legenda Aurea des Jacobus de Voragine.* Translated from Latin by R. Benz, p. 124. And: Th. Graesse (Ed.): *Jacobi a Voragine. Legenda aurea,* p. 106: «Domine, volo salvus fieri et non permittunt me cogitationes meae [...]».

his bow, until finally the archer complained that it would break. «And that is how it is in the service of God» said Antonius, «if we took on more than we could deal with, we too would soon break.»[7]

Despite leading the life of a hermit, Antonius was not cut off from the real world. At the time of the Christian persecutions around 311, he set off for Alexandria with other brothers in order to support those being persecuted, be it in the dungeon, the courtroom or at their execution. After continually removing him, but without being able to drive him away completely, the judges finally left him alone. Once the persecutions stopped, he returned to the desert. He always showed an interest in church matters and occasionally turned to the bishops whenever he deemed it necessary. But his favourite place was in the desert. Athanasius tells of an amusing episode:

At the request of the Catholic bishops, in the conflict with representatives of Arianism, a Christian theological doctrine which rejected the idea of the Trinity, Antonius once went to Alexandria to make an important speech on the subject. As they tried to keep back the seething hordes milling around him, he said that it did not bother him at all, since he was accustomed to a much larger crowd of devils in the desert.[8]

One day, when Antonius received a letter from Emperor Constantine, he reacted very calmly, almost with indifference, and it was only after the brothers persuaded him to do so that he agreed to send a short, respectful and dignified reply.[9] As he grew older, Antonius had two brothers as his servants, but otherwise the "inner mountain", as his home was called, remained a solitary place of prayer. On the mountain slope with the rock tombs, the "external mountain" of Antonius, many people had followed his example and had settled there. Occasionally Antonius would wander through the desert to talk to his pupils and receive the many people seeking advice. He did not much like having visitors at the "inner mountain". For that reason, he had a place of retreat at the top of the mountain that was

7 R. Benz (Ed.), *Die Legenda Aurea des Jacobus de Voragine*, p. 123 f.

8 L. von Hertling, *Antonius der Einsiedler,* p. 73.

9 Ibid., p. 74.

Fig. 4: St. Antonius, preaching to monks. Icon in the monastery of St. Anthony.

not easily accessible and which nobody else was allowed to enter except himself. He often spent a long time there and visitors had to wait for days, even weeks, till he came back down.

His fame spread far and wide, and many people went out into the desert to seek advice from "the Great", as he was called.[10] The faith that people had in his grave personality knew no bounds. Faced with insurmountable difficulties in life, people would finally say: «Go to Antonius; the great man is still alive», tell him about your desperate situation, listen to his advice and act accordingly, «for through him, God speaks to you». These are the words of Palladius in his *Vita Antonii*. «He was indeed a healer, sent by God to the land of Egypt. For who came to him in sadness and did not return home full of joy, who came in tears, mourning the death of loved ones, and did not immediately forget his grief, who came full of anger but departed with friendliness in his heart?»[11] From the depths of Antonius' solitude, there emerged, albeit unintentionally, a vast wealth of pastoral care. Walter Nigg referred to him as one of the greatest psychological therapists of all time.[12]

In his 105th year, Antonius laid himself down to die, having instructed his servants never to reveal the site of his grave. And in fact it has never been revealed, so no cult has been made out of his grave. It is true that later a monastery was established at the oasis, where just a few pupils had lived during his lifetime, but even in later years, it remained a place of solitude.

10 D. C. Butler, *The Lausiac History of Palladius*, Chap. 24. And: W. Nigg, *Das Geheimnis der Mönche,* p. 44. Only in very exceptional cases was the title "the Great" conferred on figures from Church history.

11 W. Nigg, *Das Geheimnis der Mönche*, p. 45.

12 Ibid., p. 46.

Fig. 5: The monastery of St. Anthony on the Red Sea.

Fig. 6: The temptation of Saint Antonius. Rudolf Stahel, Book painting.

3. The Battle with the Demons

We shall now take a further look at the life of St. Antonius, continuing to remain faithful to his own language or the language of his legends. Antonius is regarded as the founder of desert Christianity. The example he set lured countless pupils and followers into the desert during his lifetime and also triggered off a veritable wave of converts to hermit life in the desert. Young and old alike were captivated by some elemental force that was to last for almost a century.[13] Antonius' decision to go into the desert was the heroic act of an individual, contrasting sharply with the alarming spread of mass Christianity at that time. He thus embodied the contrast between the hopelessness of the man of the masses and the individual on whom alone things have always depended.[14] What he was seeking to regain was the direct link between the soul and God, which he believed could only be found in the desert. Antonius is also seen as the father and founder of monasticism. The word 'monk' means 'the one who lives alone.'[15] Thus the first desert fathers and the first monks where also 'individuals', laymen, ordinary people in no way connected with official church Christianity.

At a time when Christianity was being diluted and a general sense of confusion prevailed, Antonius struck out in a new direction, one that represented a genuine path of renewal within the framework of early Christianity. And for later generations, the life of Antonius served as a model for the rejection of worldliness in favour of a withdrawal into one's own solitude and the ensuing suffering.

A legend describes how Antonius, carried away in spirit, sees the whole world covered in slings which are all tied together. He cried out,

13 W. Nigg, *Das Geheimnis der Mönche*, p. 53.

14 Ibid., p. 51.

15 Ibid., p. 43.

saying: «Oh Lord, who can escape from all these slings?» Then he heard a voice which said: «Humility».[16]

In this modern world of ours, constantly faced with global and manifold threats, we may well feel the same and ask in resignation: «What can an individual do about this?» The response given to Antonius was 'Humility', that is, "Submit to the will of God", as Antonius would say. In other words, renounce the claim that the external situation of hopelessness can be remedied by a know-all attitude. For Antonius, that did not mean that he gave up fighting for good with all his strength if it was indicated from within. His 'Humility' however excluded the claim to power, which so often follows close on the heels of good intentions. There is probably also a need for humility when it comes to wrestling with one's inner demons, one's own unpleasant shadow side.

So Antonius returns to the desert, leaving behind the trappings of human civilisation and opts for the scene of terror, madness and death, the totally god-forsaken world, the den of Satan and all evil demons. And it is precisely here that he has his deepest experience of God, an exclusively one-to-one conversation with God. The legend tells

how Antonius, living in the rock tomb that served as his home, was set on by a horde of evil spirits with horns, teeth and claws. After much painful suffering, there appears a light, and in it is Jesus, who chases away the Devil. Antonius asks Jesus why he did not come to his aid earlier. Jesus replies: "Antonius, I was with you, but I wanted to see you fighting. And now that you have fought so manfully, I will make your name famous in all the world."[17]

Thus when he seemed to be furthest away from God, in the hostile desert, Antonius experienced God most nearly. It was only in the struggle with the demons that, according to the legend, he recognised the light inside of which Jesus had always been present. Jesus then wanted to make his name great in all the world. Indeed the influence and effect of the saint

16 Th. Graesse (Ed.), *Jacobi a Voragine, Legenda Aurea,* ch. XXI, p. 105.

17 R. Benz (Ed.), *Legenda Aurea*, ch. XXI, p. 105.

did spread far and wide, although that was by no means his intention. Despite the fact that he removed himself further and further away from his fame and his successors, venturing deeper and deeper into the desert, and although there was never any real pilgrimage centre, the cult of Antonius spread far beyond the borders of his own country across Asia to Europe. And over the centuries, his name has remained alive in the Western world right up to modern times.

If we translate the symbolic language of the legend into psychological language, to make it accessible to our modern understanding, then the abandoning of human civilisation and entering the desert, with its demons, would mean an abandoning of the ordered world of consciousness, with all its attendant conventional views and opinions. It would also mean a thorough examination of the threatening contents of the unconscious, the alarming and dark shadow figures in our dreams, the demonic forces behind our drives and our drivenness. For St. Antonius, the evil spirits haunting the desert were connected with the disposition of the person experiencing them. He actually states that the evil spirits appear to us in different ways «according to our prevailing emotional state».[18] But we cannot escape them. They tortured even Antonius to the point of actually making him lose consciousness. He recognised that the demons were somehow connected with man's psychic nature.

As we know, in Europe, wherever Christianity started to spread, the pre-Christian gods were shorn of their powers, condemned, resisted with all the resources the Church had at its disposal and kept apart from the faithful. In Alpine countries, where we can still recognize the old gods, today in archaic winter customs, in which noisy, fearsome, demonic figures charge through the villages. In Egypt, too, the pre-Christian gods became devils and demons living in the desert.

For the people of our modern civilisation, demons no longer exist. Or so we choose to believe. As the theologian and religious historian, Walter Nigg, says, this is nothing more than a typical prejudice of the age of rationalism. Although the demons may seem to have disappeared, it is only their external form that has been destroyed, not their inner reality.[19] This inner reality is the

18 W. Nigg, *Vom Geheimnis der Mönche,* p. 41.

19 Ibid., p. 38.

reality of the unconscious parts of the psyche, which nevertheless have real repercussions in the conscious life. Repressed by the Christian demand that people be good, there lurks in the unconscious everything that is not good or that at least is less good, and is thus selectively faded out of consciousness. As mentioned above, these are the shadow sides of the personality, which have an influence on the way we behave. The desert is an apt image for the unconscious itself. In contrast to the lively world of culture, it is a place of emptiness and loneliness that is hostile to life, where the unconscious fantasy world can make its presence felt and the inner demons can spring into action. Antonius seems to have been fully aware of this inner aspect of the demons.

Antonius says: «*Those who sit and repose in isolation have three battles fewer to fight: they can no longer be misled by seeing, hearing and speaking. There is just one battle left to face: against the heart.*» *And:* «*Remove the temptation and nobody is saved.*»[20]

The life of Antonius seems to illustrate perfectly that without this battle, which the individual must face completely alone, there is no possibility of discovering God, no renewal of consciousness and no religious revival. But Antonius would not be a saint if everybody were able to adopt this course of action. For a distinctive feature of the legends is that the dangers and demons facing Antonius in the desert often take him to the very brink of physical and psychological death; only his exceptional will-power and toughness enable him to escape. The battle with the demons of the unconscious calls for a firmly established self, a personality solidly rooted in life. For a victory by the demons is tantamount to an overpowering of consciousness by the figures of the unconscious. That signifies mental illness, madness, which really does lurk in the desert. This fact we have to bear in mind if we consider persuading someone to examine his unconscious despite his resistance, for 'demonic' contents in the unconscious psychological background can turn out to be a real threat to mental health.

The alchemists, who – more or less consciously – presented psychological facts and laws in the descriptions of their experiments, also projected the encounter with and examination of the shadow or

20 Ibid., p. 35.

Fig. 7: The temptation of Saint Antonius. Copper engraving.

the demons in their retorts. Their experience was surprisingly similar to that of Antonius in the desert. They described it as *nigredo*, the phase of the alchemical *opus* which corresponds to the psychological state of depression. Marie-Louise von Franz has this to say on the subject:

«In the first phase, the *nigredo*, the initial matter (*materia prima*) is dissolved, calcined, pulverised and washed or cleansed. This is a dangerous stage in which toxic vapours often develop, lead or quicksilver poisonings are generated or explosions occur. According to ancient texts, living inside lead there is "a brazen demon who can produce mental illness". The subject feels confused, disoriented, falls into a deep melancholy, or feels he has been transported to the very depths of Hell. The nigredo has its parallels in the individuation process, in the confrontation with the shadow. Everything which one has criticised in others, with moral indignation, is "served up" in dreams as part of one's own being. Envy, jealousy, lies, sexual drives, desire for power, ambition, greed for money, irritability, all kinds of childishness suddenly stare implacably at one, out of one's dreams. Illusions about oneself and the world fall apart, ideals are revealed as desire for power in disguise, 'sacred' convictions as hollow. Whenever a latent psychosis is present, Nietzsche's spirit of gravity really can lead to mental illness. The self feels deprived of its illusory almightiness and is confronted with the dark and confusing power of the unconscious This state can last for a long time, even years, till all the darknesses have been made conscious, all autonomous partial personalities (autonomous complexes) have been acknowledged and morally kept in check.»[21]

The beginning of an examination of the shadow can sometimes lead directly to a period of anxiety and depression, and fierce resistance to this path of uncertainty often needs to be overcome. Frequently there is a great temptation to abandon the whole idea and seek a solution externally. When this happens, all the blame, all the evil, no longer lie within the self but outside; it may be the State, society, the nasty teacher, the uncomprehending partner, who should be changed. Or else there is a one-sided and purely externally oriented attempt to escape from an apparently hopeless situation by changing jobs, changing partners, going on a cruise, building a new house and so on.

Antonius opts for the internal path. He seeks renewal in the desert. In today's world too, this seems to be acquiring more importance. Genuine inner renewal does not come about as a result of the security guaranteed by a state-controlled, neatly and tidily organised life. In our Western society, the greatest suffering is often to be found not in external circumstances but in the inner desert, regardless of external prosperity or the degree of social

21 M.-L. von Franz, *C.G. Jung. His Myth in our Time,* p. 222f.

care provided. But, as is shown so vividly in the life story of Antonius, that is precisely where an in-depth renewal of the individual and, ultimately, the collective attitude can take place. Antonius seeks out this desert of his own free will; he literally proceeds to his own death, going into an empty grave-like cavern, to be precise. For him, it means the beginning of a new life. He treads a path that even in his days was unconventional, but it is this that finally makes him an exemplary healer and saintly figure.

Abb. 8: St. Antonius with Devil, pig and fire. Sculpture, ca. 1490.

4. The Devil's Legends

The temptations and challenges to which Antonius was subjected by the Devil are the most distinctive feature of his life. He is often depicted with a vanquished Devil under his foot. It is perfectly conceivable – especially during his first sojourn in the desert when he had to cope with hunger, thirst, cold, heat and sexual abstinence – that he was beset with devilish thoughts: dissatisfaction with the loss of his fortune and with the challenging existence he had chosen, erotic fantasies, doubts about whether he had made the right decision in leaving the world, disappointment about the failure of his efforts to meet God and so on. Caught up in the painful conflict between temptation by the Devil and desire for God, he had to undergo suffering, he had to endure the conflict without first being granted enlightenment and without the certainty of it ever being granted. According to the legend, it was only after being half flayed to death by the Devil that Christ appeared to him in the light and relieved him of his agony. One might feel that the help could have been offered much earlier, but it seems to be a fact of life that a conflict often has to become unbearable before the intervention of a higher instance, as it were, brings about an unexpected turn of events, maybe in the form of a dream or a combination of meaningful coincidences. A solution can suddenly emerge that comes as a complete surprise and yet is so obvious, as if it had always been there and had just been "awaiting our suffering".

The following legend tells how Antonius overcame the Devil in battle and thus became aware of his true nature.

«Antonius, by the strength of his faith, had overcome the Devil, who tempts with physical desire. Then the Devil appeared to him in the figure of a black child, and threw himself at his feet, saying: "You have overcome me." For Saint Antonius had prayed to God that the devil of unchastity who pursues young people be revealed to him. And seeing him in the figure of the black child, he said: "I have seen you in your despicable form. I shall henceforth fear you no longer."»[22]

22 Benz, R. (Ed.), *Legenda Aurea: «[...] vilissima mihi apparuisti specie, te ultra non timebo.»*

For Antonius, the Devil that tempts with carnal lust would manifest in such things as the erotic thoughts and fantasies that assail the tormented body of the man suddenly plunged into utter solitude and cut off from all human contact. For Antonius, apparently it is not enough just to conquer the temptations of the Devil; he would like to find out more about whom he has to thank for that. He would like to get to know the Devil, so to speak, for he asks God to reveal him. He is seeking a greater awareness of the nature of evil, but the answer God gives him is not what he is expecting. The Devil comes in the shape of a black boy who throws himself at his feet. The sequence of events is not entirely clear in the legend, but it seems Antonius is relieved because things are not so bad after all. The devil in his 'despicable form' ('*vilissima specie*')[23] is actually a mere child, of whom he no longer need be afraid.

On a personal level, we would say today that the legend speaks about the acknowledging of one's own infantile drive shadow. Not just for Antonius, but for the age in general, the acknowledgement of this unconscious shadow was a necessary reaction to the uninhibited sensuality that was typically lived out in Classical Antiquity. Accordingly, the conflict between the devils of carnal lust and the striving for knowledge of God was at the very centre of the ascetic life of the period. Ultimately it was about achieving a moral distinction between good and evil, the chore characteristic of Christianity, which clearly distinguished it from the religions of Antiquity. At that time this seemed to be what the unconscious was striving for. It represented the civilising purpose of the Christian ideal in general, for the attainment of which in the first part of the Christian era, the light, spiritual, masculine aspect of Logos was necessary. In those days, the overcoming of pagan and animal primitiveness was the number one cultural task.[24]

If we now take a leap forward into the Middle Ages, when these legends were most widely known and the Antonius cult was at its height, we see a similar spiritual constellation. It revealed itself in many contrasts: between ecclesiastical and secular power, between Pope and Emperor, between the high moral condemnation of all sensuous drives as sinful worldliness and the misery of ordinary people, between the graceful, chivalrous game of courtly love and the sheer licentiousness which was the

23 Lat: *vilis* = worthless

24 E. Jung/M.-L. von Franz, *The Grail Legend*, p. 216.

order of the day at the courts; similarly, the ideals expressed in the greatest poems of Walther von der Vogelweide and in Wolfram von Eschenbach's famous *Parsifal* contrasted sharply with the blatant mercenary activity of the period, and St. Francis' commitment to poverty stood in stark relief against the wealth, power and corruption of the Church. All of these opposites existed side by side in a kaleidoscopic jumble, and, once again, a development towards greater consciousness was indicated.[25] It was thus that the heroic struggle against evil became central to the ideal of the Christian Knight. Antonius' confrontation with the dark powers can be seen as heroic, but Antonius was not a hero in the sense of the Christian Knight, for he lacked fighting spirit when up against the evil in the outside world. His heroism lay in engaging with great humility in the struggle with his own demons.

It comes as a surprise that the Devil in this vision of Antonius appears as a child. At first glance, we cannot understand the message of this strange image from the unconscious soul background of Antonius. We must therefore examine the general meaning of the child symbol, because it embodies an archetype that is particularly relevant and widespread. In myths and fairy tales, there are frequent references to a child who is conceived, born, and raised in exceptional circumstances. It is usually burdened by a suprapersonal, divine destiny and also has superhuman traits. And yet it is just like an ordinary, mortal child, who might be abandoned, threatened, exposed. It is pursued by a malevolent power, and yet miraculously emerges unscathed from all hazards, and will even end up as King or its equivalent. This figure of the child (or the young hero or heroine) is found all over the world and in every age with the same or similar basic features. Because it is both divine and human, it can connect the two spheres, the divine and the human. It is therefore, as Jung puts it, a contrast-unifying symbol which can connect the conscious and the unconscious parts of the personality.[26]

25 Cf. Huizinga, *Herbst des Mittelalters,* p. 191f., 257f., 151f. And: J. Fried: *Das Mittelalter.* Ch. 8.

26 See C.G. Jung, "The Psychology of the Child Archetype". In: *The Archetypes and the Collective Unconscious* [CW 9/I], § 278, § 280f. According to Jung, the collective soul has created in mythological language a symbol which connects divine destiny and human adverse fate. It is a uniting symbol, which connects the conscious and the unconscious parts of the personality and in doing so, tends to psychic wholeness. This is why it is a renovator, a mediator, a saviour, a symbol of the self.

Because of this unifying quality, the child symbol often crops up in dreams precisely when we are faced with a conflict for which there seems to be no solution. In such a case, it represents a potential solution or the beginning and the development of a whole new approach that has been eagerly sought after, only to be rejected again and again. For despite hardship and suffering, one often resists something new because one remains attached to old beliefs and views as one does to an old pair of shoes. In fairy tales and mythical tales, these outdated, threadbare beliefs are symbolised by the old King who threatens and persecutes the hero child, turns him out in the forest or throws him in the river, etc. An example from the Bible is the evil deed of King Herod, who, when the astrologers announced the birth of a new King of the Jews, arranged the killing of all the boys in Bethlehem up to the age of two (Matth. 2.16). The rescue of the mythical child finally occurs because it is a divine child with divine attributes. That would mean that acquiring a new attitude or a new insight comes from a suprapersonal sphere. *In psychological terms, divine participation corresponds to the participation that the unconscious processes have in our conscious life.* Whether or not we manage to arrive at a changed attitude or overcome an obstacle and take a new step, therefore seems to depend not only on our good intentions, but above all on what is happening in our unconscious background as well.

However the child that now appears to Antonius in his vision is black. At the time of Antonius, black-skinned people from the South of Egypt, or from the interior of the African continent, were probably ranked with the lower classes, if not even with slaves. Thus ‘black’ may simply be associated with the despised, the inferior. If we turn again to fairy tales, we find a related manifestation of the divine child who has dark features, namely the dwarves and elves. They are hidden powers of nature which may be unimpressive but can still exert a supernaturally powerful effect. The divine child thus also appears as an aspect of a pagan God of nature. In such manifestations, the child is quite ambivalent, sometimes good, sometimes bad. Only if you treat him properly is his helpful and forward-looking side revealed. If you do not get on well with him, as is common, especially in sagas, the situation can turn out to be threatening and dangerous. As we know, a real-life child also has its various sides.

The sudden, unscrupulous transformation of our angel into a little devil always has the quality of a surprising and overwhelmingly natural quality to which we cannot really do justice to with the all too rigid, moral criteria of good and evil.

If we allow ourselves to be moved by the miracle of the awakening of a child, of the emerging of something new and amazing as he develops, then we also understand why the child has become a symbol for people of something that contains within itself the potential of continuous growth and creativity. If this potential can be realised, development runs its normal course. When that is not the case, when something is not allowed to grow as it should, the natural development fails and all sorts of disturbances occur. A child whose development has been suppressed as a result of an authoritarian, psychologically narrow-minded or neurotic upbringing, often attracts the attention of those around him by behaving in an inappropriate or aggressive manner, just as a tooth in a too narrow jaw will inevitably force itself out, painfully and in the wrong place. The same applies to the contents of the unconscious and to any potential that a person may have, which their consciousness will not accept because it appears threatening or disturbing. Where such unconscious contents turn up in the symbolic form of a child, it suggests either something infantile, an attitude that is too childish, or else a new creative content, a creative potential for a new future.

In the legend of the black child, Antonius fought the Devil, "which tempts with carnal lust". The physical drives and particularly sexuality are something for which no solution has ever been found within the framework of Christianity since Antonius. The ecclesiastical authorities have widely condemned sexuality as diabolical and even our mothers can tell incredible tales about how common it was in their youth for anything to do with love and sexuality to be suppressed. It needed a Sigmund Freud to liberate this side of life from its taboo. However, it was then turned into an object of a rational materialism and thus devalued, the negative effects of which can still be observed today in many ways. In the course of this development, sexuality came to be seen as the banal object of performance, consumption and commercial marketing. Furthermore, the removal of the taboo around sexuality did not solve the problem of the *relationship* between the sexes. In fact, initially it made it worse, for with a purely materialistic attitude towards the whole question of sexuality, people ran the risk of lapsing back into an unconscious 'animalistic' state. The danger of losing the ability to act like a human being, of losing ego consciousness, was depicted in the myth of Odysseus and his companions, who were changed into pigs by *Circe*, a negative Nature mother. So the problem is not a new one!

For Antonius, the whole question of sexuality was connected with the Devil. The symbol of the child brought in a new and surprising aspect. It seemed to be indicating that the problem of our instinctual drives needed to be approached in a different way. The legend implies that the black child as an aspect of the Devil is a manifestation of his powerlessness, and so Antonius no longer need fear him in this despicable form. This idea corresponds to the thinking at the beginning of the Christian era, which started to separate light and dark and, as a result, favoured a purely light image of God, splitting off everything evil and placing it in the sphere of the Devil. However, if the legend describes the Devil as a black child, it imparts to him the divine quality of the child symbol. In his blackness this child seems to complement the light side of the baby Jesus. Thus, at the very beginning of the Christian era, the black child could have been pointing to a possibility of a holistic image of God which did not exclude any aspect of human nature. In the perception of Antonius, however, the black child was unacceptable. By underestimating it and thus overcoming his fear of the Devil, the problem of the instinctive drives was apparently solved for him, as appeared to be the case in Christian thinking for a long time, until the black child seemed to return later on in other forms.

Initially, however, as Jung pointed out in *Aion*, up to about the year 1000, the emphasis lay totally on striving for the light of Christ and on the spread of Christianity. From then on, there were growing signs of an unusual change in the spiritual sphere, manifesting itself in the emergence of various religious movements, such as the Holy Spirit movement, the new Manicheans, Cathars, Albigensians, etc. and finally in Western alchemy.[27] These movements concerned themselves with the problem of evil, of the nature of the feminine and of the divine within the individual, in a manner which sought to provide what had hitherto been lacking in Christianity.

27 C. G. Jung, "Aion", In: *Aion* [CW 9/II], *§ 235.*

Fig. 9: Binding and Releasing of the Antichrist. From the Bamberger Apokalypse, after 1000 AD. This miniature is the only known image with this theme, as it was mentioned repeatedly at the turn of the millennium with its expectation of end time.

However, the main distinguishing feature of their pronouncements was their chaotic symbolism and incomprehensible metaphor, and so they were attacked by the Church as being the work of the Devil. Towards the end of the first Christian millennium, the coming of the Antichrist was also expected, the domination of the evil antagonist.

Blackness and darkness are always an indication of unconsciousness, for what we cannot see remains for us in the darkness of the unconscious. The blackness of the child may therefore be linked to the fact that it could not be recognized and accepted by the prevailing consciousness as part of a new image of God or wholeness and therefore had to be conquered. In a certain sense, this brings to mind the present conflict between theology and depth psychology. It is a known fact that the former still fails to embrace the concept of a new image of God in man and thus hinders the renewal of our spiritual and religious life. Throughout his life, Jung campaigned against the prejudices of the theologians, who, although they generally showed great interest in his findings, ultimately could not accept them. The one-sided image of a "loving God", preserved by the Church as a metaphysical truth, still encourages us to denigrate a large portion of human nature, without helping the good in us really to break through. The psychological consequences of this Christian legacy are still not generally acknowledged.

The central message of the Church, which still influences the thinking of every person in our Christian culture, even if he describes himself as totally irreligious, is that God is not only omnipotent, but is also good and loves us. We therefore cling stubbornly to the notion that the divine will should attend to our well-being. "Dear God, please ensure that..." is the basic tone of each urgent prayer. But if He is omnipotent and His being is pure love, where do all the human misery, evil, and the cruelty of nature come from? There is no answer to this question, a question raised by Jung at the beginning of *Answer to Job*. However, the god-image has persisted, and it has bequeathed to us a Christianity with a separation of good and evil. In most religions, and particularly in tribal cultures, there is no such clear separation. There is an unquestioning acceptance of the fact that everywhere there is good and less good and there are Gods that are decidedly malicious or fearsome. The Christian separation of a good God from a bad Devil has brought us a more conscious distinction between good and evil, but today we realise that this has not helped us to rid the world of evil. We do not really know how to deal with it, neither in the outside world, nor within ourselves. The Antonius legend of the black child does, however, seem to indicate that there is such a thing as a divine child in the psyche which is able to reconcile these terrible contradictions.

According to Jung, the child, who is, in fact, the epitome of constant growth, represents «the strongest and most inevitable of human compulsions, namely self-realisation [...]. The urge to self-realisation is natural law and is hence of insurmountable force, even if its effect is initially insignificant and improbable.»[28] The child therefore represents a nascent state of consciousness, a symbol which remains a mythological figure, or a religious projection, or else a projection onto any outer circumstances, as long as man cannot recognise that it is an internal reality, not an external one. The child represents the new in the positive or negative sense, what man should – but cannot yet – be or do.[29]

The child symbol paves the way for a future change in personality, not only on a personal level, as can often be seen in dreams. In connection with our legend of the black child, it suggests a change in the God image, in the collective attitude towards religion. What kind of God image will it be? Where will evil fit into it? And how will people be affected by it? We can see that there is a dimension to this Antonius legend that has far-reaching consequences, even if at the time, in its black appearance, the child could only be seen as an object of something to be despised, its potential going unrecognised. Could it be for this reason that, in accordance with the legend, Christ had wished to witness the battle of Antonius? Could it be that in this legend's strange statement, we are being told that within the psyche itself there is an interest in the outcome of the confrontation between the opposites and in their potential reconciliation within a new wholeness? This new wholeness would not be a regression into the old, undifferentiated, unconscious state, but rather something completely new.

No doubt there are also legends and dreams in other religions which point both to the renewal of a god-image that has become inflexible or has lost all its meaning, and also to the renewal of what it means to be a human being. But as we are products of a Christian culture, and – consciously

28 C.G. Jung, "The Special Phenomenology of the Child Archetype". In: *The Archetypes and the collective Unconscious* [CW 9/I], § 289.

29 Ibid., § 287.

or unconsciously – are formed and shaped by it, and as my dream had chosen a Christian Saint, we shall here trace the path of such a spiritual development in the sphere of Christianity.

In the three legends which come after the one of the black child in the *legenda aurea* collection, the Devil appears in the form of a giant demon. This is the first legend:

«The Devil seemed to him (Antonius) so big that it looked as if he was touching the sky with his bead. Antonius asked him who he was. He replied: «I am Satan and I would like to know why the monks are against me and the Christians curse me. Antonius said: «they do it so readily because they are much grieved by your cunning.» The Devil replied: «I don't grieve them at all, they grieve each other. But I have been destroyed because Christ rules in every country.»[30]

The black child figure of the Devil may have seduced Antonius into underestimating his power and effectiveness. So the Devil does what all underestimated and despised contents of the unconscious eventually do. He becomes huge. Whereupon Antonius asks him who he is. Today, in exactly the same way, one could ask any such threatening figure from the unconscious – be it in a dream or in a so-called active imagination – what its intentions are and what it means.

The Devil now complains in an almost naive way about being rejected by monks and Christians. He is far from content at having been 'displaced' by Christ and his unilateral rule. The background to this legend is the fact that in the Old Testament, Satan had his function as an opponent not only of the Almighty, who was omniscient and good, but also of the angry, unjust, unpredictable God, the legend of Job being a case in point. The idea that Satan and Christ were the two opposing sons of God can even be found in the early Jewish-Christian Church.[31] Only later, as Christianity evolved, did Satan become the actual Devil, responsible for all the evil in the world. God, on the other hand, lost his Old Testament dark features and came to embody the highest good from then on. *Deus = summum bonum.* From this, Christian thinkers developed the idea of *privatio boni*, which has had a strong influence Christianity: «All goodness from God, all evil

30 Benz, R. (Ed.), *Legenda Aurea.*

31 C.G. Jung, *Aion* [CW 9/II], § 103.

from Man». In other words, as God represented the highest good, only Man could be responsible for evil.[32] Jung shows in his work *Aion* that this idea had – and still does have – psychologically far-reaching and dangerous consequences. He points out that, on the one hand, it overestimates human nature, whose goodness in reality is often not enough even to outweigh evil, let alone to bring about its disappearance, while on the other hand, it also holds Man responsible for the survival of evil in the world. Jung formulates the psychological consequence as follows: «If this paramount power of evil is imputed to the soul, the result can only be negative inflation – i.e., a daemonic claim to power on the part of the unconscious [...]. This unavoidable consequence is anticipated in the figure of the Antichrist and is reflected in the course of contemporary events [...].»[33] *Aion* came out in 1951, only a few years after two terrible world wars.

The following legend reflects this negative inflation either by the forces of evil or the temptation to make use of this demonic power

«Antonius himself said: I once saw the Devil in the form of a giant.» He even dared to call himself the power and providence of God and asked me: "What do you want from me as a gift, Antonius?" I looked him in the face and hurled myself at him, armed with the names of Christ, and he immediately vanished.»[34]

The gift of the Devil is the temptation to bestow divine wisdom upon oneself, so to speak; it implies an obsession with power in which the Devil as the dark side of God is in the background, pulling the strings. Antonius, however, "turned on him strongly" and drove the Devil away. Today, it is not so easy to get rid of such a 'devil shadow'. He wants to be acknowledged and listened to in his whole demonic greatness, for he is the embodiment of a superhuman reality that can cause serious trouble at all times and in all places. In this respect, 9/11 was just one ominous sign, and the conflicts erupting all over the world today are its continuation.

A clutching at power on a large scale, a devilish inflation, is also behind the sheer presumptuousness of our modern culture, to claim the

32 Ibid., § 94 f. "*Omne bonum a Deo, omne malum ab homine.*"

33 Ibid., § 114.

34 Benz, R. (Ed.), *Legenda Aurea.*

whole world and to exploit and, experiment with it, interfering with the processes of nature, always apparently with the good intention of improving the lot of mankind. But we all know that other significant factors are often involved, namely power, money, selfishness, ruthlessness and egocentricity. This collective shadow problem, as the driving force from the realm of the unconscious, is powerful, as the Devil's appearance before Antonius illustrates, and it has not diminished over the last two millennia. Today it is on the way to destroying the very foundation of our lives. This may be the reason why evil seems everywhere to be able to assert itself more easily than goodnesss, despite the fact that everyone claims to be seeking only goodness. It is not easy to resist the temptation associated with the dark influx of power from the collective unconscious. The greater the lack of consciousness about the origin of this temptation and the stronger the one-sided striving only for goodness, the greater the danger. This is particularly easy to observe in the realm of politics and with public policy makers of all kinds, but it is also seen on the personal level, whenever the real motivations behind seemingly good intentions are kept in the dark.

Another aspect of the devil shadow is expressed in the following legend:

«Antonius had once been questioned by some brothers about the state of souls. The next night, a voice called and said: «Stand up, go outside and look.» And behold, there was a great and terrible man who raised his head up to the clouds. With outstretched hands, he was trying to hold back winged creatures who wanted to fly up to Heaven; but some flew freely on and he could not hold them back. Antonius heard cries of joy, mingled with cries of lamentation. Then he realised that this was the ascent of souls, and that the Devil was holding back some who were enslaved to him, and the cries of lamentation were from him if and whenever he was unable to curb the saints in their flight».[35]

This legend tells us how Antonius is questioned about the fate of souls. The vision he receives on this subject is not in accordance with

35 Benz, R. (Ed.), *Legenda Aurea.*

Fig. 10: The vision of St. Antonius. Basilika Sainte-Madelaine, Vézelay Burgund.

Christian tradition, which might state, for example, that perhaps God or Peter would be responsible for the entry into Heaven. Instead, Antonius is shown a terrible figure who hurls the souls enslaved to him back to Earth or even – according to a later interpretation – sends them to Hell. Only the Saints or the good souls get away from him and fly on to Heaven. The lamentations of the Devil over the preference given to the saints recall his grief over his fall from power (in the previous legend), but now it is much greater. As we know, the *imitatio Christi*, that fervent striving of the saints for Christ-like light and grace, creates a huge shadow in the unconscious by way of compensation, revealing such manifestations of the Devil as is the case here, and many had to struggle with this. With today's 'saints' the Devil manifests himself in such things as moral judgements, which assign to Hell the sinners who have not chosen the path of the saints. A self-righteous devaluation of all those classified as 'less holy', as can often be seen where so-called 'good people' are working to improve the world. They may become so intransigent in their convictions that they have no hesitation in adopting brutal methods to bring down sinners, i.e. their opponents. In this case, the end apparently justifies the means.

Today, we can see that at all times, the work of the devil shadow was always grimmest where people felt most confident about being on the side of the good. We can recall all the terrible things that happened in the name of the Christian God, the many wars of religion over the centuries and during the conquest of foreign countries and peoples in the name of 'Christian' kings. It is similarly not hard for us now to see the work of the Devil behind the high-minded conduct of the medieval Inquisition. Today, however, in a period of general religious decline, the devilish shadow manifests in new ways.

Christian efforts to do good are still always justified and necessary and, on the collective level, "sociably acceptable". But at the same time, wherever evil is projected, one is attacking one's own shadow in the other person, and the Devil ends up with more power rather than less. The less one knows about one's shadow, the more devilish characteristics it has. It is precisely where one gives the impression of having only the best intentions that the shadow draws attention to itself in the form of more or less malicious actions. But this need not necessarily be the case, for: «it depends on ourselves whether the shadow becomes a friend or a foe. [...]

He will only be hostile if you treat him insensitively or ignore him.»[36] The shadow has to do with dark traits or inferior characteristics, usually of an emotional nature. The more unconscious we are of the shadow, the more easily it gets caught up in emotions and affects that are difficult to control. So it often wrecks the most beautiful plans and upsets the apple-cart when it is least expected. The shadow is always throwing a spanner in the works, frustrating other people's well-intentioned projects and laughing up it's sleeve when each new, supposedly great achievement leads to a whole series of unexpected, destructive side-effects. The cause of these problems is then repressed – a real vicious circle! But "I only meant well" is the plea, when things have gone wrong. Thus, the opportunity is missed to catch the shadow red-handed, to nail down certain hidden, selfish motivations and desires, to recognize excessive sensitivity or to acknowledge failure to relate to others.

Let us return again to our first legend, in which Antonius asks the Devil who he is, whereupon the latter declares himself to be a very sad devil, who objects to the fact that Antonius holds him responsible for all the evil that people have to cope with. «I don't torment them at all; they torment each other.» In actual fact, Antonius' judgement of good and evil is being questioned here. The devil resents being blamed for all the malice in the world and passes the buck back to the people themselves. Following the discussion above, we can understand this to mean that it is ultimately up to each individual to decide the question of good and evil. So we are back to the problem of the shadow, the projection of which attaches to people who seem to be what is unconsciously part of ourselves. In this case, it puts up unexpectedly stubborn resistance to moral scrutiny and is particularly difficult to recognise.[37] In our legend, the Devil himself is the projection-carrier. Following his advice to withdraw the projection and to accept evil as a personal characteristic is an outstanding moral achievement for the ego. Usually, the personal shadow is not really evil; it is simply a matter of inferior characteristics which exist along side the conscious personality, but are given little or no attention by the ego. These

36 M.-L. von Franz, "The Individuation Process". In: C. G. Jung, *Man and his Symbols,* p. 171.

37 C.G. Jung, *Aion,* § 16.

traits are not absolutely evil; they simply want to be part of the package, sometimes more, sometimes less. In dreams, they may appear as different species of animals, for example. Where animals are involved, there is usually an element of vitality and instinctiveness, which may also have positive value. We shall come back to this in connection with the pig. When it comes to individual shadows of this nature, a rigid assessment on the basis of good and evil is not always the right approach. There is needed, above all, an awareness of and a willingness to deal with the shadow characteristics. These characteristics may only really be black as a result of being repressed and could actually be quite helpful as part of the conscious personality. On the other hand, even the best intentions can give rise to a dark shadow, with the result that they have a bad effect. Sometimes, it seems, the collective judgment of good and evil needs to be relativized. However this statement seems to be fraught with danger, for how can a society function without collective guidelines and laws that apply to everyone? And what about the above-mentioned 'immoral' mixing of opposites?

Ultimately, the best guidelines, rules and laws are only effective if there is still such a thing as a personal sense of responsibility in addition to conventional prescribed morality. For a kind of innate inner sense of right and wrong seems to exist in the human psyche, a general, human, emotional or value judgement which determines the guidelines for the individual. It can be equated to the voice of conscience, manifesting itself from the unconscious base of the personality. As Jung points out, a distinction must be made between this individual conscience and the so-called moral conscience, which is determined through custom and external law.[38] The autonomous, original voice of conscience was in earlier times referred to as *vox Dei*, in other words, as direct manifestation of the divine. This issue will be dealt with again in the chapter on the Bell. Such a manifestation of the unconscious background, as seen in dreams, for example, has an effect on the individual's appreciation of good and evil. It can initiate a continuous weighing up and appraising of what is manifested from the unconscious. This has nothing to do with any form of subjectivism. For if, in the best scenario, one manages to wait for – and understand – the reaction of the

38 C. G. Jung, "A Psychological view of Conscience", in: *Civilisation in Transition* [CW 10], *§ 825-857.*

unconscious, this can lead to a more critical and at the same time more tolerant attitude not only towards oneself, but also towards others.

But we now know that distinguishing between good and evil – not only at the time of Antonius – was an essential phase in people's collective, mental development. It can also be seen in the development of the consciousness of every human being. If we observe a child, we may see that one day, without any intervention on our part, it begins to deal with this very question of good and evil. Then it is fascinated by the 'bad' boy or the guy next door. And it is not just in the Punch and Judy show that the first fierce fighting goes on, between the Devil and Caspar, Knights and Rogues, Cops and Robbers, but also among the children themselves. To the horror of parents, swords and toy guns are at the top of their children's wish list. In this phase, fantasy characters of any kind are strictly classified into categories of good and evil. This is an important step in the child's development. Thus it moves gradually further and further away from the natural, animal-like, unconscious state in which it dozed through its infancy. However, this natural unconscious is permanently poised to regain what has been newly acquired. Consequently there will inevitably be frequent states of regression, relapsing again and again into the old unconsciousness, not only in the development of an individual child, also in the intellectual development of the people; all the knowledge that has been gained will seem to have been lost again. We have already hinted at this process in relation to the myth of the endangered hero child.

Thus the unconscious inner nature always presents a threat to the newly acquired consciousness as well. This is true even today, for there is still an unconscious dark area of the collective psyche that meets with strong resistance. Not only for the early Christians, but also for the people in the Middle Ages, anything at all that related to nature was threatening. Sexuality, in particular, and generally everything associated with the sphere of the feminine nature mother was rejected as hostile, evil and of the Devil. We need only recall the witch trials, in the course of which, innocent girls, mothers and old women were tortured, burned and killed, because they had been accused of having dealings with the Devil. In fact, it was often women who were particularly beautiful and attractive – or who otherwise stood out from the crowd – who fell prey to male fanaticism. The splitting off and exclusion of so much of the natural feminine sphere of life in those days has had far-reaching consequences for us today. In the long term, this problem cannot be ignored. It has a strongly disruptive effect which and the more we turn a blind eye, the more threatening it will become. On the other hand, it represents immeasurable potential for renewal and development, as we saw earlier in the symbol of the black child. In fairy tales, which reflect the unconscious, collective background of an era, the theme of the split-off feminine is everywhere, but the possibility of its resurfacing is also hinted at. M.-L. von Franz was the first to carry out a comprehensive study of the treasure trove of fairy tales, from our culture and others, based on the psychology of the unconscious.

Oddly enough, even in the first centuries of Christianity there was, running parallel to Christianity itself, a secondary spiritual movement, one which tended more towards reconciling the archetypal opposites of human nature rather than separating them. Probably at about the time of Antonius the hermit, namely in the 3rd/4th century, the first historically documented figure in Greek Alchemy – the great alchemist *Zosimos of Panopolis* – was living in Egypt. *Zosimos* was close to the Gnostic hermetic understanding of the world, which, like Christianity, was also gaining ground at that time in Egypt.[39] The focus here was on the veneration of the 'inner Godman', which reconciled within itself the areas of conflict of the pre-Christian gods, areas which, as we have seen, had become demons and evil spirits in Christianity itself. So alongside the growth and development of Christianity in Egypt, alchemy pursued its own independent course. In his writings, *Zosimos* explains to his pupil *Theosobeia* his thoughts and experiences, which – in contrast to the early Christian separation of the opposites of good and evil, nature and spirit, male and female – tended towards a union of these opposites. Alchemy thenceforth led its own separate existence over the centuries, usually excluded from the Christian Church on the grounds of heresy. C.G. Jung was the first to point out its importance for our time, thus making its incomprehensible symbolic language accessible to modern psychological thinking. What Jung discovered in alchemy, to put simply, was a symbolic expression of the uniting of those very psychological opposites which Christianity had torn asunder and which, still today, cause us to project our own unconscious dark side externally, so we see the Devil mainly in others.

39 Th. Abt, *The Book of Pictures, Mushaf as-suwar,* CALA II, 1., p. 9-11.

Although this separating of psychological opposites was taking place at the time when St. Antonius was leading his ascetic desert life, his courageous confrontation with evil made him a personality with an exceptional aura, a figure who made a deep impression on people. He took the devils and demons seriously and did not project them onto other people or circumstances. He was able to internalise or integrate them to a certain extent. Probably unintentionally, he placed them where they belonged and where they came from, namely in man's suprapersonal psychological background. This enabled him to become a role model as a individuated personality who set himself the task of confronting his inner demons and devils, without becoming overwhelmed and possessed by the archetype of evil.

The confrontation with the archetypal powers of the collective unconscious is dangerous because they are above and beyond the personal. The holy hermits made the withdrawal from society that was essential if these powers were not to be projected, and they were careful enough not to become addicted to them; it was also important for them not to become inflated by the projections of others. For even in his own lifetime, Antonius was worshipped as 'the Great', and his image came to resemble more and more closely man's notion of the Anthropos, the mythical figure of cosmic man, the eternal, universal human archetype. According to Jung, this notion corresponds to the self, the greater inner personality of each man and the collective soul.[40] For it is also this projection of the self which gives exceptional people the attribute and the power of holiness.

Today, hermits have become as thin on the ground as rare species of animals. But these ancient figures from the past still stand as role models. Now, more than ever before, isolation and introversion need to be defended against the pressure of an extraverted world. For the necessary confrontation with the devils and demons – those powerful archetypes of the collective unconscious – has shifted today to the inner emotional level of each individual. Only there, in the individual, and not in the masses, does an awareness of what is going on in the background become possible. A genuine, ethical attitude can only come about through an individual, subjective examination of the inner psychological opposites. This process is essentially different not only from largely fighting against evil in the

40 M.-L. von Franz, *C.G. Jung – His Myth in our Time*, cf. "The Anthropos", p. 122–138.

outside world and in other people, but also from blaming the whole burden of evil exclusively on the inferiority of the human individual. An inner conflict of this nature may perhaps be able to break through the toing and froing between human hubris and resigned hopelessness in which human consciousness has become increasingly ensnared as in our first Antonius legend.

In summary, we can say that in the legends of Antonius there already seem to be signs of an inner spiritual reconciling of archetypal opposites. In what now follows, we would like to look at how this process can also be recognised in the attributes that people have attached to this saint over the centuries. How do these attributes describe to us the effect of the divine opposites in human nature? How do these contrasts affect us? What does the confrontation with them actually mean? We now turn to the fire, the pig, the bell and the cross, circling round them with the possible ways of understanding them opened up to us by contemporary depth psychology. In so doing, we shall see that in a certain way the symbolic attributes of St. Antonius fit into a meaningful context.

5. The Fire

Between the lives of saints in the desert in the third century and the altar images in a modern European Church, there lies a lengthy period of history which we shall now briefly outline. This will give us a better understanding of how Antonius comes to the attribute of the fire in our initial image. Sometimes on altarpieces, on reredos, in relief works or on carved figures, he also carries a torch or a bundle of brushwood or a vessel containing fire, or he is actually standing in the fire. Imagery of fire is rather less frequently found than of the pig, but according to the legends, and especially after the medieval importance of Antonius as a healer of the so-called 'Antonius fire', fire has been an essential feature of this saint.

An archetypal image or icon can surface anytime, anywhere, from the unconscious background to the human psyche, and nowhere can a psychological fact of general significance find better or more comprehensive expression than in this symbolic form. Today the symbolic language from the time of the saints appears to have little or nothing to tell us that we could relate to our lives. We have largely lost access to it. Medieval altarpieces are often now of only aesthetic or artistic interest, with any deeper meaning of their symbolism having apparently little connection with modern life. With the hypothesis of the collective unconscious, C.G. Jung has revealed an important way – probably one not yet fully appreciated – of opening up this old symbolic language to our modern-day understanding and of making its precious spiritual and intellectual content accessible again. This discovery extends well beyond the scope of psychology and affects all those areas of life in which common human forms are visible. If we consider fire as a symbol, which we can enrich with other archetypal material from mythology and intellectual history, we can see a deeper meaning which would otherwise have escaped us.

So what is the connection between St. Antonius and fire? Let us recall first the development of his cult. Antonius, who was publicly venerated soon after his death in the Eastern Mediterranean, was one of the most popular saints in early times. By the 5th century veneration had

Fig. 11: Saint Antonius with pig. 1468.

spread from Constantinople to the West.[41] Legend has it that his bones were found at a later date and his cult received fresh impetus when these relics were transferred to Europe around the year 1000. The cult reached its zenith in the late Middle Ages, above all in the 14th century, but was still alive even up to the 18th century. In Switzerland, the worship of this saint is still going on, especially in the mountain areas, where Antonius has become the patron saint of agriculture of domestic animals.

When, according to legend, the relics were moved to St. Didier-de-la-Motte in France, the order of the Antonites was founded by Gaston Guérin, a French nobleman, in grateful thanks for the fact that his son had been cured of 'Antonius fire' or *ignis sacer*. This was a plague-like disease which broke out in the Middle Ages. It began with a burning reddening of the skin and was probably caused by the consumption of *Ergot*, the poison of the Mother-corn lurking in the crop. Whereas in the East, Antonius was worshipped primarily as a hermit and founder of monastic communities, in the West he was viewed rather as a miracle worker and a patron of the sick. The order of the Antonites was established to care for the poor and particularly those suffering from Antonius fire.[42] Antonius was also called on to deal with the so-called 'swine erysipelas' or 'pigs erysipelas', a bacterial infectious disease still common today in domestic animals, especially pigs, but also in humans. This disease was also referred to as the "fire of St. Antonius". Such diseases represent the most obvious link between Antonius and fire. We shall come back to this in the chapter on the pig. But why precisely was it Antonius who became the healer of these diseases?

Here we must ask how the fire symbol is related to the healing power of the saint. We may consider in this connection the ideas of certain archaic tribes, according to whom, fire is in the possession of the medicine man.[43] He is responsible not only for the healing of the sick, but also for dealing with the spirits and demons that cause the diseases. Antonius, fighter of demons and medieval healer, thus bears shamanic traits. As regards fire itself, we have to search more deeply.

41 H. Aurenhammer, *Lexikon der christlichen Ikonographie,* p. 158.

42 Ibid., p. 158.

43 A large collection of fire customs can be found in J. G. Frazer, *The Golden Bough.*

Fig. 12: Niklaus Manuel: St. Antonius healing the sick and the possessed.

Generally speaking, in popular belief fire is one of the most important elements, found to have a therapeutic and apotropaic effect. In Switzerland, for example, sick children used to be carried to and through the smoke of St. John's fire. In many places, you had to walk through or jump over fire to ward off diseases or cure them.[44] Flames and coals of fire consecrated at Easter were regarded as protection against any harm, including disease and sorcery. The so-called emergency fire, which was ignited particularly for the healing and prevention of livestock diseases, had special significance. Easter fire and emergency fire had to be lit mostly by drilling or friction, i.e. by drilling a hole through wood on wood, until the resulting spark ignited an easily flammable material such as dry grass or sticks; in other words, in the same way as when fire was first ignited in primeval times.

In folklore, we see different traditions where this original drilling for fire is still ritually carried out. Using matches would obviously now

44 Hoffmann-Krayer, *Feste und Bräuche des Schweizervolkes,* p. 152. Also: *Handwörterbuch des deutschen Aberglaubens,* vol. II, column 1400f. and cf. J. G. Frazer, *The Golden Bough.*

be a simpler way of making fire, but it would not carry the deep symbolic meaning embedded in the old rituals. So we have to consider the symbolic importance of creating fire. Jung states that the rite of fire drilling, that is, the creating of fire in the primeval way, represents a symbolic recollection of the emerging of human consciousness and its enlightening and redeeming significance.[45] Figuratively speaking, the direct source of fire is matter. Linguistically, the Latin terms for wood and mother – *materia* and *mater* – are related.[46] Unknown matter, the most comprehensive image of the maternal unconscious, potentially carries fire within itself, so to speak, and through the fire it destroys itself. In other words, the wood, the old unconsciousness, is burned up. Psychologically, the springing up of the spark of light from matter signifies the possibility of renewal and the possibility of the growth of consciousness from the unconscious. The ritual use of the original method of creating fire was a highly symbolic gesture, expressing significant psychological facts. It must have had a satisfying effect on the people of earlier times, so much so in fact, that it did not need to be examined further. Today we attempt to understand the symbolic aspect of the old custom in psychological terms, for it contains intuitive knowledge of the ancients about spiritual matters, knowledge that has been lost to us in this form. However far-fetched it may seem, if we amplify the fire of Antonius in this way and connect to him, the figure of the Saint thus becomes clearer, gaining in both depth and meaning.

Antonius is presented as standing in or over the fire, so for the observer he must have a special relationship to fire. Apparently there is nothing that can harm him. There is no misunderstanding what the phrase means if someone "has gone through fire". But anything that goes through fire is somehow always changed. There has always been the notion that in fire, anything that is unclean is burned up and ascends to the skies purified and transformed. A case in point is the rite of sacrifice to the gods in fire. In animal sacrifices, for example, the physical is burned and reduced to ashes. On the level of the psyche, this symbolic act also means sacrifice of animalistic drives such as hunger, thirst, sleep, sexuality and emotional states, i.e. the affects connected directly to the physical. For Antonius, all

45 On fire and the symbolism of fire-making: C. G. Jung, *Symbols of Transformation* [CW 5], § 240ff., § 248ff.

46 Wood in latin: *lignum*, wood to be worked upon in latin: *materia*.

this smacked of the Devil. His fire sacrifices were a manifestation of his ascetism. From this we can already see a link to the symbol of fire.

When man began to make fire, it was, like the acquisition of language, an incredible discovery that gave him an enormous advantage over animals. Not only could he now cook his food and warm himself by the fire, but fire also provided him with light, and hence the ability to detect things in the dark. The significance of this development in the evolution of mankind, can be seen in those myths where the acquisition of fire is depicted as a robbery or theft by man or animal from the gods. For with the discovery of how to produce fire, man had, so to speak, snatched a secret from Nature itself. That is why, in Greek mythology, Prometheus was punished so severely for stealing fire from the gods to bring to the people. But the theft brought human culture, with new ways for people to protect themselves against the menacing forces of nature and to asserting themselves in the world. Later, in a similar way, as we have seen, fire came to signify the higher knowledge of the medicine man or saint, which could exert power over evil spirits and hence over disease and death.

Thus, it is not just the victory over the destructive fire, or its sacrifice, that is presented in the fire symbol of Antonius, namely the overcoming of torrid passions, affects and impulses, inspired by the Devil, it is also the potential to achieve higher consciousness. Even if, for Antonius the Devil was the embodiment of all that is evil, he is, as the name Lucifer suggests, (in Latin *lux, lucis* = light, *ferre* = bear) also a bringer of light. It is true that in the form of the treacherous serpent, he brought Adam and Eve into conflict with God, which led to their expulsion from Paradise, but, in this way, he also brought them self-awareness. This concept says that realisation, enlightenment, consciousness can be brought about by the Devil. But just how does this double meaning of evil or of fire work in the psyche?

Jung formulates it as follows: the Devil is a perpetual instigator of conflict, which is actually a Lucifer virtue, because ultimately, it is precisely conflict that can lead to increased awareness. «Conflict generates the fire of affects and emotions, and, like any fire, it has two aspects, namely generating light and burning. [...] Emotion is actually the main source of all development of consciousness. There is no conversion from darkness into light, and lethargy into motion, without emotion.»[47] Often it is only in some emotional conflict which was not consciously sought, but which steps in uninvited from the unconscious, that we begin to become aware of an underlying problem. Only our involvement, our dismay, and the heat generated by effort and emotional arousal, can provide us with the warmth necessary for the incubation of the problem and finally bring illumination, a new perspective, a new point of view, a new approach to dealing with the problem. A small, new light of consciousness has emerged from the fire, and from the ashes, a tiny grain of gold.

Ultimately, it always boils down to the question of balance between opposites. If the aspect of burning becomes predominant in situations where emotions are running high, the aspect of the generating light is lost. As is the case in baking, where too much fire burns the bread or the cake, so it is that the unimpeded fire of passion – be it hatred, love, jealousy or the fierce desire for something that you cannot obtain – can wreak havoc in our lives. But as in baking, heat is needed and so the inner fire must not be extinguished, fiery emotions must not be suppressed, if psychological transformation is to be achieved. Unless there is emotion, we are not moved, no lively interest is aroused and so, nothing new happens, no light goes on, there is no development of consciousness. The heat must therefore be regulated, kept within limits, tamed and endured, so that finally it can produce a transformation. Fitting symbols for the struggle to regulate the fire can be found all over the world, in all cultures, always pointing to the need for the too violent reaction to be sacrificed. Let us recall how easily both archaic and modern man can be overwhelmed by rage, leading to murder and manslaughter. In the ritual of the fire sacrifice, viewed symbolically, it is the venting of rage that is being sacrificed, even if it threatens to choke one internally, or one feels no longer able to stand the pressure. If one succeeds in enduring the fire and is able to "sit and roast in hell", then finally «the fire is extinguished with it's own inner measure», as an alchemical text expresses it, and the lapis, the philosopher's stone, is brought forth. The unconscious then, as pure nature, can then establish its own inner balance.[48] Christian teaching requires us to suppress the fiery

47 C. G. Jung, *Psychological Aspects of the Mother Archetype*, in: *The Archetypes and the Collective Unconscious* [CW 9/I], § 179.

48 M.-L. von Franz, *Alchemy,* p. 252f.

emotion. To suppress and to deliberately sacrifice are two very different things. The first violates human nature and increases the risk of an uncontrolled outburst; the second offers the possibility of transformation and psychic development.

A fiery and passionate love will also eventually force one to make a kind of 'fire sacrifice', so that a deeper relationship can evolve, which would be able to survive in a permanent flame, instead of ending up as a pile of gray ashes. Passion, with that famous butterflies-in-the stomach feeling, always seems to be merely a preliminary phase, albeit a necessary one, but in the ensuing ups and downs of everyday life, it must or can change into a genuine relationship, hardened in the fire. If the other party in a relationship increasingly exhibits characteristics that seem strange and difficult to tolerate, one starts seething inside, heated arguments break out, and then one ends up in hell-fire instead of the dreamed-of paradise. Passionate love can easily turn into a hatred that is no less passionate. When such problems crop up, then the animus and the anima are always involved as unconscious participants. Since in any human relationship, these two are responsible for the most violent outbursts, it makes sense to examine them more closely. These terms, which Jung distilled out of his experience, and which he clarifies and explains throughout his whole work, are an invaluable tool in the understanding of psychic processes. M.-L. von Franz summarises this as follows:

«If the conscious personality has been more committed to the Logos aspect of life, as is usually the case with men, then the Eros aspect appears personified in feminine figures in dreams. Conversely if the Eros aspect of life has received more attention from the ego, as is general the case with women, then there will be masculine personifications of the Logos aspect. Jung called theses contrasexual personifications of the unconscious personality the *anima* (in men) and the *animus* (in women). In a man the anima finds expression principally in the form of specific positive or negative moods or feeling tones, of erotic fantasies, of impulses, inclinations and of emotional incentives for life; while the animus of a women will appear rather in the form of unconscious impulses to action, sudden initiative, autonomous babbling, opinions, reasons or conditions.»[49] And in somewhat different words: in its positive aspect,

49 M.-L. von Franz, *C. G. Jung – His Myth in our Time,* p. 70.

the anima is also «feminine empathy or sensitivity, sometimes also the sense of feeling, eros artistic tendencies, love of nature, acceptance of the validity of the irrational. Negatively, it is moodiness, irritability, subjective judgment, whininess, hypochondria, sentimentality. The animus in a woman manifests positively as initiative, depth of thought, consistency, courage, sense of religious truth; negatively as rigid opinionatedness, brutality, exaggeratedly masculine behaviour, and so on.»[50]

Animus and anima are now not simply mental templates that are responsible for certain patterns of behaviour; they act as clearly defined, soul images, appearing specifically as certain male and female figures in dreams and fantasies. The more a partner corresponds to this inner image, the stronger the fascination. Accordingly, the starting point for relationships is the soul image which each partner sees in the other. However, in reality, difficulty arises, because it is often the case that the partner has very little in common with the inner vision, which was cast over him or her like a veil. Here we have the phenomenon of projection; it is similar to the way we can project the image of a wonderful South Seas Beach onto a room wall, but underneath the image there is still nothing more than our blank wall. For an onlooker, especially in the early stages, a passionate love affair usually has an unreal quality about it. "How can he or she just...?", is what outsiders and know-alls ask. The answer is that, as a result of this projection of animus and anima, the connection is based on a common unconsciousness, which only becomes a problem if animus and anima in their less attractive forms begin to cross swords. Then things really get heated, and attraction and repulsion can enter the relationship with equal intensity. If what has been projected onto the partner can be withdrawn without any loss of feeling and the warming fire is not extinguished, and if the real personality subsequently becomes more and more visible, then there is the basis for a relationship which can survive future storms. The relationship has then passed the fire test, even if the darker side of the partner, not so much one's own, of course (!), can again and again cause problems. Whether such a baptism of fire is successful, sometimes seems to depend not on goodwill alone, but simply on fate. Ultimately it depends on how far the irrational effects of the anima and animus can be detected.

50 M.-L. von Franz, "Individuation and Social Relationship in Jungian Psychology," in: *Archetypal Dimensions of the Psyche,* p. 364.

In other words, this developing consciousness of the animus and anima in men and women signifies the union of the conscious ego personality with the contrasexual parts of the soul. However, it is possible only with the help of what we might call "regulated fire"; that means ongoing emotional affection. Where a problem does not concern one, there is no change. That would be too little fire. On the other hand, the strong emotions always associated with animus and anima must not escalate into open fire, for then one loses control and also loses touch with reality. This is a sign of animus or anima obsession. Jung explains that: «in a state of obsession, the two figures lose their charm and their values, which they possess only in their isolationist (introverted) state, divorced from the world, i.e. when they form a bridge to the unconscious. When the anima turns its gaze outward it is unpredictable, excessive, moody, lacking in self-control, emotional, sometimes demonically intuitive, ruthless, untruthful, hypocritical and mystical; the animus, on the other hand, is inflexible, rigidly principled, lays down the law, didactic, world-improving, theoretical, gets entangled in words, is quarrelsome and domineering.»[51]

If the animus or anima appears in the partner, one's own unconscious opposite number will at once swing into action. Depending on the situation, one becomes angry, aggressive, spiteful, undisciplined or emotional. Arguments will ensue if one fails to discipline one's own animus or anima, if one is unable to remain calm and to postpone the confrontation or – which is most difficult but most effective – to defuse the situation with humour. For where animus and anima have the upper hand, there is usually nothing to laugh about.

In whatever way mankind has explained the origin of fire, it always has the aspect of a force of nature from the Beyond, a force that is not man-made. For example, the fire is often in the possession of a god from the chthonic world such as *Hephaestos*, the lame blacksmith and Greek god of volcanic fire, a dark deity, working away in the earth or, like the Nordic trickster god *Loki*, revered as the lord of fire. The Indian God *Agni* embodies fire itself. The word *agni* is related to the Latin *ignis* = fire. Sometimes a primeval mother is also in possession of the fire. Loki himself even appears as a witch-like woman or as a giant woman in a mountain cave.

51 C. G. Jung, *The Archetypes and the Collective Unconscious* [CW 9/I], § 223.

In the sphere of Christianity, too, there is the idea that fire is divine in origin. If we return to the roots of our Christian image of God in Old Testament times, we come across its original fire aspects. *Jahweh* did not just appear as a huge column of fire, but also possessed all the dangerous, destructive characteristics of fire such as rage, anger, violent affect, heated emotion, self-righteousness. These qualities make it extremely difficult for us to explain the notion of a 'Loving God' to our children on the basis of the Old Testament stories! *Jahweh* only had the attribute 'loving' bestowed upon him in the Christian era. Only then did he become the benevolent father and lose the fiery traits of his character, which were then assigned to the Devil instead. But this development also entailed removing from the image of God the warm emotion, the feeling side that also belongs to fire, and it includes the indiscriminate, chaotic, feminine side of God. We find these traits in our culture in fairy tales, for example in the Devil's grandmother, who hides the hero away and prevents him from being eaten by the Devil. With Christianity, fire became hell-fire, merely for roasting sinners, and its enlightening, warming aspects were lost.

However, as Jung has demonstrated, the fire aspect of God can still be found in a non-canonical saying of our Lord which runs: «He who is near unto me, is near unto the fire!» Christ as a source of fire is also shown on a glass window from the church of Königsfelden in Switzerland. In connection with alchemical symbolism, Jung says: «The source means not only the flow of life but its warmth, indeed its heat, the secret of passion whose synonyms are always fiery. The all-dissolving *aqua nostra* is an essential ingredient in the production of the *lapis*. But the source is underground and therefore the way leads underneath: only down below can we find the fiery source of life. These depths constitute the natural history of man, his causal link with the world of instinct. Unless this link be rediscovered, no lapis and no self can come into being.»[52] What this means basically is that any 'enlightenment' or illumination, any psychological development in the sense of individuation, cannot come about without the painful dissolution of hardened views, opinions and beliefs and without enduring conflict. What gives rise to this 'dissolution' and conflict-ridden state of affairs, is the fiery source from below, the instinctual, emotional background of the unconscious, which in certain circumstances can

52 C. G. Jung, *Psychology and Alchemy* [CW 12], § 157.

Fig. 13: Saint Antonius, standing in the fire. Ceiling sculpture, Parish church in Trier.

frustrate our best intentions and upset our usual goals. But in this way, the contact with the fiery energy of the unconscious is established, even if again it is not without the danger of possession.

As long as we are smiled upon by life, we are seldom prepared to confront the strange phenomenon that so much of what we do is not actually based on our own decisions, but seems instead to be determined by an unknown factor. Only if we are, for example, the victims of an accident, illness or other difficult life situations and are confronted with unexpectedly violent emotions and feelings, do we suddenly recall the old prayers of our childhood. The fiery God in the unconscious puts us in jeopardy, inflicts illness, excessive heat and burning. On the other hand, such an experience also means hope, the possibility of renewal, of new light, of overcoming depression. Apparently it is only through a major life experience that a conscious connection can be made to the unconscious instinctual basis, to what makes up our life and what influences us from behind the scenes. We are forced to acknowledge that there is someone else living in our house and to see all that he might be responsible for. That is why the fire of emotion must be maintained, until it transforms itself to provide the illuminating light of deeper insight and greater consciousness. If we seek to extinguish the fire of emotion, of anger, hatred or love, despair or self-accusation, either out of self-pity or pity for others, it jeopardises the process of developing consciousness, which cannot be achieved without this passionate fire. The devil and hell-fire in the service of individuation!

The psychological facts expressed above are probably what lie behind the biblical saying about it being easier for a camel to pass through the eye of a needle than for a rich man to enter the Kingdom of Heaven, it being generally understood that a rich man has no grounds for suffering. The quotation below can be seen in the mortuary chapel of Unterschächen in the canton of Uri:

"Man dich in dem Feuer gefangen halt bis du den letzten Haller gezahlt.

Niemand in Himell wird geführt Er werd zuvor durchs Feuer brobiert."

What this says basically is that one should be kept in the fire till one has paid the full price, and that nobody can be allowed into Heaven without passing through the ordeal of fire.

Although not attributed to Antonius himself, this meaningful phrase shows us the medieval Antonius in an unusual light, not just as the bringer of the "Antonius fire" but also as the healer of this terrible plague-like disease. The psychological truth behind this symbolic statement is that where there is disease, healing can also be found. Suffering must apparently be endured until the inner wholeness of a personality can emerge, whose consciousness is able to unite the destructive and the enlightening aspects of fire. In a tale from Malaysia, the hero, who is named "The half", is thrown into the fire, where, like a piece of metal, he is hammered into a whole being. With this dramatic image, the tale portrays the archetypal hero's fate of agony, death and transformation so that finally the real self or a higher consciousness can emerge.[53] The half becomes a whole, a complete person, who is connected with his other half, his own, unconscious fiery nature, without being destroyed by it.

The relationship with this other half, i.e. with the unconscious and the whole realm of drives and impulses, is frequently troubled in a person whose mother lacked a natural, instinctive motherliness. This disturbed relationship is most evident today in the field of sexuality, and expresses itself, for example, in the childish attitude which attaches a similar importance to sexual satisfaction as to dealing with hunger and thirst. A lasting, conscious relationship cannot develop from this attitude of a spoiled or neglected child, because a child throws away his toy as soon as it starts to annoy him. The child runs away as soon as difficulties arise. The fire of passion dies down before any potential transformation can be realised.

An unconscious content seeking to become conscious can be compared to the fall of a river. There is energy in the movement of water which can be converted into some other form, such as electricity. In the original production of fire, energy is also converted, namely from movement into heat. The ritual of making fire, which itself is later of no practical importance, symbolically represents the important transfer of psychic energy or libido into consciousness. Where this cannot come about, there is congestion. This means that the river of life ceases to flow, the sense of *joie de vivre* and vitality declines or there is depression. It is therefore of the utmost importance that anything that is pushing to break free from the unconscious and achieve consciousness can actually do so. In a neurosis, conscious life is so sharply separated from the unconscious that the congestion makes its presence felt through disturbing notions, fears, thoughts and ideas. Life can no longer flow along in a natural way and the congestion needs to be cleared away. The libido that has built up in the unconscious, the fiery river of life, must be transferred over to consciousness in carefully measured doses, which means not simply opening the flood-gates in order to live out everything that had been previously repressed and had therefore caused the problem. In analysis, dreams often help to determine the measure in which the fiery power may be supplied to consciousness.

53 H. von Beit and M.-L. von Franz, *Symbolik des Märchens,* p. 371.

Where the warming fire, the energy, has gone from life, there is a great temptation to seek vitality and movement through every possible form of diversion, leisure activities, travel, dangerous adventures, mass events and, in recent times, the feverish virtual world of the Internet. If we look at a World Championship football match on television, where tens of thousands of excited fans are awash in an overwhelming, collective flood of emotion, we can witness this tremendous, fiery flow of energy which would be alarming if, thank God, it did not have this outlet. When life in this industrialised, totally rationalised world of ours becomes grey and colourless, then there is a yearning for new energy, new fire. This yearning is also what lies behind the way people turn to drugs, for example, for by dismantling conscious barriers, drugs seem to facilitate a turning to the "lower man", to the energy-laden contents of the unconscious. Dependency and addiction, however, are nothing more than a constant controlling of consciousness from the "fiery source from below". The danger lies in a destruction of the conscious personality, a burning down of the house, of a person's conscious ego structure. In such a case, the unconscious need to come into contact with the fire aspects of life carries more weight than the price that has to be paid through mental and physical destruction.

Sometimes we are cast into the fire by life itself, maybe because of an unfortunate love affair or some other difficult conflict, a situation that could get out of control because there is no apparent solution, or an overpowering obsession that could get out of hand. Deeply stirred, we then defend our feelings and opinions as if they were "sacred convictions". They come from the archetypal level of the psyche, which is the basis of their claim to higher validity. Always and everywhere, therefore, the question is how to deal with fire, with this unconscious source of energy, in both its destructive and constructive aspects.

We occasionally feel wonderful if we give free rein to a genuine outburst of rage; we thoroughly enjoy our anger, even if we have to pick up the pieces afterwards. That is why, if we are honest, we might feel that it can be fun to be part of a mob smashing a large shop-window. At last we feel we are as one and feel definitely alive. If we have suppressed an aspect of our personality for too long, weather to fit in with others or for the sake of convenience or owing to external circumstances, it accumulates energy in the unconscious and pressure builds up. If we open the flood-gates suddenly, as can happen in a fit of temper, the flood waters are released. The unconscious takes control. If there are many people together, overwhelmed in this way by the unconscious, the whole thing is increased by the force of the mass and it spreads like wildfire. We can see this kind of eruption of energy from the unconscious in the dangerous dynamics of street demonstrations; on a larger scale, it leads to war and rage.

The Christian Church has largely excluded "the lower part", matter, the unconscious, which is the bearer of fire and energy, by unrealistically demanding that people should repress their inappropriate, weak, dark, evil sides, should conquer nature and the body and just concentrate on being good. The question did not arise as to how one might deal with these "negative" sides, the idea being that they should simply cease to exist. The less you were aware of them, the sooner you could imagine being able to meet the demand for goodness. Even though today most people imagine that they are not much influenced by Christian thought, the repression of the "lower part" of our human nature is still remarkably common and, undetected in the unconscious sphere of the psyche, it frequently causes trouble. Christian instruction has taught that fire belongs to the Devil in Hell. According to popular belief, he can be seen as "the red one", dancing in the flames of a burning house. Today, we see him in the fire of violent and uncontrollable emotions bursting forth from the unconscious. Consciousness, particularly of an intellectual kind, does not recognise the psychological causes of this fire, but constantly looks for external factors to explain it. Many people feel helpless in the face of the destructive anger of young people, the increase in brutal crime, the rise in terrorist acts by fringe groups, as well as of general undermining of traditional values and morality. There is a modern perception that God has handed over His authority to the State, so let them get on with it. Thus the State is given excessive power over the individual, without being able to quench the dangerous fire.

To reach a better understanding of the roots of this development in Christianity, let us go back to the time when Antonius abandoned his familiar way of life and moved into the desert to devote himself to the fight against demons. Some seventy years before Antonius, the Christian martyr Perpetua lived in North Africa. M.-L. von Franz wrote about her at great length in her essay *The Passion of Perpetua.* She describes how at that time there suddenly surged forth from the unconscious a strong spiritual

Fig. 14: St. Antonius: Devotional.

emotion in the form of a passionate conviction, which made its way into consciousness like a powerful force of nature. Perpetua married young and was the mother of a little baby when newly acquired strong Christian convictions led her to leave her family and choose a martyr's death. She was executed in Carthage around the year 203. A new image of God, a new source of life came into being in Christian doctrine, not just for Perpetua, but for many people at that time. «If the ancient gods were already dead – that is, if the highest value bestowing life and giving it meaning had sunk at that time into the unconscious and become dissolved – this value had risen again in a changed form in the figure and teaching of Christ [...]. The unconscious life force streamed forth from the new teaching, enabling life to progress on a fresh course and bringing about a new step forward in culture.»[54] From the deeper layers of the collective unconscious, there emerged a spiritual change that forced its way into the consciousness of the individual like a mighty river. This early Christian period was, as M.-L. von Franz explains, characterised by a powerful surge from the collective unconscious. As could be seen in the visions of Christian people, the path led upwards, meaning that the collective unconscious was striving for an awareness of the light aspect of the unconscious.[55]

As we have seen, this new spiritual development led to a splitting of the God image — the image of the one almighty father split into that of a son and a dark opponent, into Christ and the Devil. M.-L. von Franz goes on to say that psychologically this constituted a splitting of the unconscious psyche, namely into 'top', associated with what was constant, ordering and ordered, light, good, masculine, intellectual and so on, and 'bottom', associated with what was dark, evil, feminine, compulsive, devouring, fruitful and chaotic.[56] This separation of up and down is a mythical phenomenon, found in many cultures. Our own creation myth tells of an initial separation, namely of Heaven and Earth, above and below. At the same point, M.-L. von Franz says that the splitting is a psychic process, «in which the double aspect of the unconscious itself gradually shows itself in the light of human awareness.» Perpetua was called on to repudiate the 'bottom' and thus her life as a woman and as a mother, while positioning

54 M.-L. von Franz, *The Passion of Perpetua,* p. 35.

55 Ibid., p. 69.

56 M.-L. von Franz, *Passio Perpetuae* (German Version), p. 34.

herself on the spiritual side. For her and for the representatives of the early Christian period in general, including Antonius, there was no other way; they had to respond to the fiery river from the utmost depths of their being, even at the cost of their lives. The upwelling of such a powerful call from the unconscious initiated a new universally valid, psychological situation. The reaction of people was a moral one, namely a unilateral commitment to the bright side of the now divided image of God. Later, as we have seen already in the devil legend of Antonius, this striving for the light was to lead, by way of compensation, to the rise of the repressed opposite the dark side. The anticipation of the Antichrist indicates that this compensation was to be expected, says M. L. von Franz.[57] We recall in this context the black child from the vision of Antonius.

Appreciating the problem of the unconscious splitting that has characterized the Christian era, may help us to understand why the political ideals of our time – which aim at the liberation of the 'lower people', i.e. improving the lot of the poor and the working classes – have spread across the globe with all the force of a new and fiery, religious idea. Viewed symbolically, the 'lower man' belongs to that repressed side of the human psyche and corresponds to the dark side of the image of God. That is the reason not only for the powerful force of the Socialist ideology that burst forth from the unconscious in the last century – another 'fiery' power – but also for its destructive potential through possession and fanaticism, a lethal threat to psychological freedom and individual development. However, today this ideology has adopted a sort of Christian morality, concealing the destructiveness of this one-sidedness and promising people that their good behaviour will be rewarded by heaven on earth. Only in this way is it possible to understand why such an ideology is still alive and continues to grow, despite the fact that it has so far failed all over the world, has created new oppressors, reduced countries to misery and caused endless suffering to people. Socialist thought combined with Christian morality is a particularly toxic mixture of superior pseudo-religious attitudes. Such an ideology is nothing more than religious fanaticism, a fiery potential, which in reality means power and war, poverty and destruction. The current parallel to the Middle Eastern crusade of Islamic 'holy warriors' and other Jihadistic terrorist organisations immediately springs to mind. It

57 M.-L. von Franz, *The Passion of Perpetua*, p. 69.

is essential that such a fire be controlled and contained, and not allowed to spread unimpeded.

M.-L. von Franz writes about the problem of uncontrolled fire: «The religious spirit in the collective unconscious is like a fire; but fire in concrete reality spells destruction [...]. There is therefore a need to find a container that can contain the fire. The first such container in which one can safely handle such a fire is *human relationship*: for even relationship to the collective is rooted first of all in individual relationship. That is why the problem of Eros is of such decisive importance today.»[58] When young people and established representatives of the older generation are in violent conflict, even then it seems to be all about the question of a new form of relationship. For relationship is the vessel which can contain the whole fiery destructive potential for violence, anger and aggression and turn it into positive energy, light and warmth. Let us therefore examine more closely the important symbol of the vessel, which belongs to the iconography of Antonius, where the fire is shown burning in a container.

The vessel was probably one of the very first cultural acquisitions. It allowed people to take, store and cook food and liquid. Cooking means transforming, making edible, assimilating. The alchemists cooked their ingredients and knew all about the life-giving and yet destructive power of fire. The form in which they sealed this fire, the alchemical oven or the *vas hermetis*, was therefore the focal point for their efforts. Like a cooking pot, the alchemical vessel was the site of the transformation of substances. Furthermore it had the significance of something wonderful, a kind of uterus with a divine content, and thus a mother symbol from which the philosopher's miraculous stone is born. This container therefore symbolises the womb of spiritual renewal and rebirth. The youth- and life-giving, wonderful vessels in mythology also have this significance. Moreover, they often have healing powers or owning them provides strength and wisdom. In medieval mysticism, the vessel was described as the image of the soul which receives divine grace.[59]

The most famous vessel preoccupying the imagination of the Middle Ages, was the Holy Grail. According to the Grail legend, it was the goal most sought after by the Knights of King Arthur, and countless

58 M.-L. von Franz, *C. G. Jung, His Myth in our Time,* p. 156. My marking.

59 Ibid., p. 251, «Oddly paradoxical is that the vessel and its contents are identical: fire, water, Mercurius and the Lapis itself.»

Fig. 15: Saint Antonius and Saint Agate. Altarpiece, chapel of Meien (Kt. Uri, Switzerland).

legendary traditions and literary works have sprung up around it. What is special about this legend is that it was connected with a Christian legend and thus no longer reflects just basic human problems, but also «depicts dramatic, emotional events which form the background of our Christian culture [...],» says M.-L. von Franz. The precious object was perceived as the vessel in which Joseph of Arimathea had collected the blood of Christ during the descent from the cross. This vessel contained, so to speak, his soul substance, the living aspect of the dead God that never dies.[60] The idea of blood surviving in the Grail means that in times when God seemed to be dead, he still lived on, albeit in a different form. The Grail is a feminine symbol, a womb, a symbol for the unconscious psyche, birthplace of all that is new.[61]

M.-L. von Franz continues: «He [Christ] survived his own death by retreating into the lap of the unconscious human psyche from which he came. The vessel and the divine substance that it contains are the symbol of a psychological attitude and experience, in which everything religious is experienced in the individual and nothing more can be seen in the external forms. Nothing more is projected onto pictures or rituals or an institution. For then it has again become the personal, overwhelming experience of the individual human being. At this moment, the dead God has returned into the vessel from which he comes back as what he always was, an immortal psychic reality. This is why the symbol of the vessel containing the essence of God has survived in later Christianity.»[62] This is true even though the ideas of the Grail legend were rejected by the Church because of their individualistic elements and for a while were even condemned as blasphemy.

Today, for many people, God is apparently dead, and we live in a time when the message of the Church is less and less understood or is regarded as less and less relevant to life. Yet centuries ago, in the myth of the Grail, the fantasy of medieval man created an antidote to this bleak, religious isolation. Throughout the Christian era, by means of symbolic images and figures, there have been additions and extensions to the faith institutionalised by the Church. This imperceptible process has occurred, also through the evolution of church customs, through the constant changing and adapting of the dogmas, and finally through outstanding personalities both within and outside the Church, including saints like Antonius. The counterweight to an all too rigid Church was and is the individual

60 E. Jung and M.-L. von Franz, *The Grail Legend,* p. 9f. And: M.-L. von Franz, *The Golden Ass,* Chapt.12, p. 11.

61 M.-L. von Franz, *C. G. Jung, His Myth in our Time,* p. 271.

62 E. Jung and M.-L. von Franz, *The Grail Legend*, p.123.

experience of something overpowering and divine in the human soul. That is where the image of god can become real, an inner reality that acquires a meaning no longer found in the stereotypical Church sermons today. The individual experience of God provides a new connection with the inner, fiery source of life for the dried out, post-Christian consciousness. It is in the psyche of the individual, in the dynamic continuity of psychic activity, that this revival can come about, says M.-L. von Franz.[63] However, the fire needs to be contained. The figure of Antonius, which sometime is depicted with a vessel containing fire, could point to a developmental process in the collective unconscious that is gradually moving the image of God away from the metaphysical realm and into the individual human soul.

Until recently, the dogmas and rites of the Church have been the vessel which enabled the faithful to deal with the fiery contents of the unconscious. «One thing is certain – that modern man, [...] has largely lost the protection of the Church walls painstakingly erected in Roman times and constantly reinforced, and because of this loss, has approached the zone of the world-destroying and world-creating fire. Life has become faster and more intensive. Our world is shaken and penetrated by shafts of restlessness and fear.»[64]. Jung wrote this in 1939. It could also have been written today.

Today, where the loss of the protective walls of the Church is a banal reality, we often observe a kind of alternative, substitute "anything-goes religion", a chaotic mixture of wisdom from all over the world, interspersed with intuitive pseudo-knowledge. In the worst cases, this jumble of beliefs combines with inflationary therapeutic and "setting the world to rights" intentions, which may violate the psychological reality of those who receive 'therapy', distorting their judgement with truths and opinions plucked out of thin air. Metaphysical claims aimed at the objective reality of the psyche completely miss the point; the fire is not contained and it threatens mental destruction instead of religious renewal. People with a weak ego soon fall under the spell of such false 'healers'. On the collective level, whole nations and groups can be captivated and overcome by such a fire.

63 Ibid., p.159. See the chapter "The Central Symbol of the Legend: The Grail as Vessel", p. 113–142.

64 C. G. Jung, "Psychology and Religion". In: *Psychology and Religion: West and East* [CW 11], § 82, § 84f.

Antonius, like Perpetua, was a personality in his day who paved the way for a renewal of the understanding of God. By adopting the path of the individual, he grappled with his inner demons, with his own nature. He lived in the desert on nothing but what came from within him, so to speak. Apparently he succeeded in finding for these fiery experiences the spiritual vessel in which they could be changed into something new, into a new conception of what God or Christ meant for him. Antonius' experience of God 'nourished' not only him, but also his many students and the people who sought his advice. It turned him into a genuine healer.

The Grail vessel, the vessel of the soul substance, is a dispenser of an unusual and inexhaustible supply of nourishment. We are familiar with the fairy tale motif of the pot that never empties and of the table always laden with food, which come as a blessing or may give rise to serious problems if not dealt with correctly. The Grail similarly has to be handled carefully. Like the alchemical vessel, it has a fire nature and even just looking at it closely is highly dangerous. The Grail legend tells how Lancelot in his search once came into the Grail castle where, attracted by a bright light, he saw the sacred vessel in a room on a silver table. As he entered, a hot breath of wind blew in his face, so much so that he thought it was burning. He lost his hearing and sight; he fell down as if dead, lost his tongue, and went for twenty-four days and nights without speaking and without being able to move.[65] Lancelot's naïve curiosity leads to disaster. The divine, fiery spirit in the soul vessel, the hot breath of wind, demands awe, caution and a respectful distance.

These descriptions in sagas, poetry and fairy tales, of a mythical vessel containing a superhuman or divine essence, clearly point to a general or archetypal idea, for it has emerged from the unconscious in many places and at various times. It is highly dangerous to approach an archetype in a naive way, failing to recognise its destructive side. Consciousness can get lost in the process, and unconscious dynamics can take over the reins. There is always the risk that we may be captivated by an archetype, becoming its slave, or being possessed by it. Any kind of obsession means being carried away by an archetype. For example, anyone who deals in depth with the archetypal dimensions of the unconscious, runs the risk in a special way of becoming inflated. The fiery nature of the archetypes

65 E. Jung and M.-L. von Franz, *The Grail Legend*, p. 146.

is always potentially both destructive and renewing. Wherever certain beliefs are no longer flexible and can no longer be questioned or discussed, we can discern the influence of an archetypal power. An archetype that is activated in the outside world is always dangerous because it affects the powers of judgement of the conscious individual. Today, for example, it is the archetype of wholeness which, for us in the West – and not just in the minds of many politicians – constantly gives rise to the fantasy of ever larger political structures without the ensuing, disadvantages and dangers being recognised. The concretising of such archetypal fantasies in the outside world is mostly associated with intolerant, dogmatic blindness and loss of reality.

Owing to the fiery nature of the archetypes, preoccupation with the unconscious psyche in psychotherapy can conceal a real danger. Many people instinctively feel that they are on shaky ground, even at the mere thought of the reality of the unconscious. However, since in our overly-rational world, there is great need for a psychological dimension, many people enthusiastically experiment with various modern psychological techniques, which promise emotional experiences and new life energy via short and speedy procedures. If these procedures remain on the surface of consciousness and hence have little advice to offer, then nothing further happens. Sometimes a quick success occurs but, since it was probably due largely to the power of suggestion, it usually fades away sooner or later. But where deeper, unconscious things are torn open because the dangerous side of the archetypes projected outward in a naive way has been underestimated, there may be a threat to mental health. This is especially true if there is no relationship, no vessel there to contain the kindled fire. If the person receiving therapy is released from the "Sensitivity Weekend", for example, he may lapse into a deep depression because his consciousness cannot cope with the fiery, psychological energy released, or 'creatively' process the new content. The vessel needed to contain what has been stirred up from the unconscious would be the soul itself, in the form of a dream, for example, through which the intention of the self and what it has in mind for the individual could perhaps be grasped.

This brings us to the connection between the vessel and creative work, in which a new idea, a creative concept, might somehow be implemented. This is a creative process can be compared to carrying and giving birth to a child. The vessel as a womb symbol, signifies carrying something around, incubating a content, until it can be assimilated, and then made tangible and brought into reality. Without a vessel, the new idea simply remains hanging in the air. A painter, for example, often carries around within himself a creative possibility, an initial inner image or pictorial idea. Then, with all the limitations of technique, materials, etc., he has to try, to the best of his ability to give it expression, however 'intangible' it seems to be. If he succeeds, he has grasped a mere spark of the fire, but it is a spark that radiates the power of the whole fire. He has brought a tiny portion of psychic truth down to the ground level of human consciousness and that is his creative achievement. Jung often encouraged his analysands to paint their dreams and fantasies, as he himself did, in order to provide the unconscious processes with an outlet for expression. Unfortunately, there is usually strong resistance initially, because people feel that they can never reproduce the colour and richness of unconscious images and that their inept painting is not really creative work. But creative work is actually only a matter of drawing on the abundance of what is already present in the psyche, without being too selective and resisting the temptation to do too much, and without striving for perfection and falling into inflation. Wherever human consciousness acquires new knowledge, only a small spark of fire is removed from the unconscious; it is inevitably selective. Even scientific work often entails excluding everything that does not conform to established hypotheses. It can only shed light on partial aspects. As long as we are aware that any knowledge can only be partial knowledge, balance is maintained and the vessel fulfils its function.

Today, however, the boundless possibilities of the age of the Internet have led people to believe that ultimately everything can be made visible and knowable; this is an alarming inflation, which carries the risk of a collective conflagration due to the fiery nature of the archetypes. The vessel of relationships has been lost in the anonymity of large numbers. Today many things in virtual space seem to develop autonomously. Unimaginable amounts of data about everything and everyone circulate in cyberspace. Not only does this omnipresent knowledge increasingly destroy the privacy of the individual, but it reduces the individual to being a mere particle in the mass, caught up in developments that he neither knows

Fig. 16: Antonius with the torch. Johanneskirche Osnabrück.

nor cares about. The danger of a regressive destruction of the freedom of the individual and of individual consciousness can no longer be ignored.

Let us return to Antonius. The torch, which sometimes replaces the vessel in pictures of Antonius, is an important element of his tradition. A torch involves selecting and taking a limited amount of fire from the whole and carrying it away. Traditionally torches used to be carried across the country in processions and parades with the idea that they would drive away demons and promote the fertility of the fields. In contrast to the passive, all-enveloping vessel as a female symbol, the torch has a more active, masculine quality, in the sense of "carrying the spark on" to start a fire somewhere else. This more active dimension may be a subtle reference to the fact that new efforts of consciousness must constantly be made so as not to extinguish the spark but rather to kindle the fire of the spirit, there being always such a tremendously strong temptation for us to lapse into unconscious lethargy. The illuminating torch, which leads to the awakening of consciousness, is thus also a torch of freedom, liberation from any unconscious constraints. And here is where the shadow comes in. It probably needs a portion of male dynamic or focused attention to shed some light on our own shadow.

In dreams, the shadow is often represented by figures which are unappealing or "not like us" or with which we otherwise have a negative relationship. These shadow puppets are, of course, what we avoid, preferring to leave them in the unconscious. Our reluctance to face the qualities of our personal shadow is due, in part, to the fact that the Devil can easily stick out his nose from behind them, for the contents of the personal unconscious are not immediately distinguishable from the archetypal contents of the collective unconscious. As the shadow becomes conscious, it takes these contents on board, as it were. Acknowledging the shadow can thus mean taking on more blackness than we are personally responsible for and this can lead to depression. It is not easy, then, to believe that the cure is to be found in the same threatening unconscious, for example, in the dream. But that is precisely the symbolic message of Antonius; he is both the bringer of illness and the healer. This paradoxical nature is ascribed to many saints. They all embody the ambiguous spirit of the unconscious, which can cure the very illness it caused!

In contrast to the feminine vessel, the torch is a phallic, male symbol. Its fire represents a piece of fiery nature that has become conscious, an item of knowledge which is able to illuminate the dark unconscious. It makes sense that in this way, fertility, meaning new spiritual growth, creativity, new life, can come into being. The 'demon-resistant torch' also helps us appreciate the superior power of the unconscious. If someone is faced with the risk of sinking into despair and depression, it helps to know from experience that a little flame from the unconscious fire can be grasped, if perhaps a dream is understood and acted upon or if a complex is recognized for what it is and accepted, then a little light can ignite in the darkness. In this way, confidence in the ability to deal with life's problems can slowly grow and the conscious viewpoint is gradually consolidated. The vessel and the torch make the medieval Antonius a bringer of culture, pointing the way to a new, spiritual way of life, nurtured by the fiery source of the unconscious soul.

If we look at the fire of Antonius in the context of the original challenges and temptations presented by the Devil, it seems as if the union of the diametrically opposed light and dark aspects of life faced by the hermits in the Egyptian desert was already being hinted at in the fire symbol. Such a union of opposites can only come about when their conflicting nature has become conscious, and when the 'hellish' suffering that inevitably follows has been endured. This process would represent a development beyond the basic Christian idea that we should promote goodness and kindness with all our strength and combat evil. Today, we are forced to admit that trying to follow this teaching, first formulated 2000 years ago, has lodged us permanently with the irreconcilable opposites of obsession with, and projection of, the unconscious shadow. We are only rarely conscious of the true nature of these opposites and of their psychic roots. Antonius, in his battle against the demons, "went through fire", but did not allow himself to be overwhelmed. He was able to grasp and endure his own fiery nature, so that the fire became for him the source of new life. As an archetypal figure, St. Antonius with the fire embodies the potential in the human psyche for psychological functioning in this exemplary fashion.

Fig. 17: Saint Antonius with two pigs. 1520/25.

6. The Pig

When I first heard about the "Säuli-Toni" or the "Sew Antoni", as our mountain dwellers call him, I was surprised. A saint and a pig in a relationship of trust and confidence! Such an unusual and amazing appreciation of the pig by a saint made him very appealing. When I was a child, pigs did little more than vegetate on the concrete floor in the darkest corner of the farm; today they lead an even more miserable existence as living abattoir meat, kept away from the public eye, penned up with hundreds of others in the cramped conditions of industrial scale production. Our children usually only see pigs now in books or movies; it is not easy to show them a living pig.

Despite their reputation, pigs are extremely clean animals. If they are looked after properly, they keep their sleeping quarters unsoiled, and their wallowing in mud is not just for pleasure, but also helps them cool down, because, like dogs, they cannot sweat. Their rooting around in the earth can be useful for a farmer if he wants to prepare ground for planting vegetables, though, of course, the nocturnal burrowing of wild boar in fields and meadows is less appreciated in the world of agriculture. The intelligence of pigs compares favourably with that of dogs, and there are many stories about them being sensitive and friendly towards people, when they are kept in healthy farm conditions. As a sow can bring 10 to 20 piglets into the world, she is considered the epitome of fertility. In the Christian view the pig has become a symbol of sinful carnal lust and dirt. Linguistically, the pig generally comes off badly. We have such phrases as 'the place is like a pig-sty', and 'pig-headed', which for us are decidedly negative! Christian ideas have contributed to the derogatory tone of these remarks.

No reference can be found to a relationship with pigs in the life story of St. Antonius. This pig symbol must therefore have been added later in people's minds. An example just how easily the topic is dealt with in the imagination of people is a folk legend from the Mediterranean

Fig. 18: Pigs wallowing in the earth.

region. It tells how St. Antonius, with the help of the pig, brought fire from Hell and drove the Devil to despair! Here we have an unprecedented but meaningful connection between Hell, fire and pig! It is said of Antonius that he was on good terms with animals in general. Legend has it that the desert animals obeyed him, and when he had to dig the grave of St. Paul, a lion came along to help him. And let us not forget that in his battle with the demons, he courageously wrestled with his own animal nature.

In our part of the world, even up to today, the function of Antonius as the patron saint of animals is at the very centre of his cult in many places. This is surprising, given that the general view of the Church is that animals have no soul and so any relationship with animals in Christianity is virtually meaningless. The reason for this view has its roots in Hebraic prehistory, but it has probably always applied to all the Abrahamic religions. «The Hebraic tradition tends [in contrast to archaic human animal worship. Author's note] to go to the other extreme. The reason perhaps, was not any impulse toward cruelty, but simply that the new monotheism was aware how easily deep concern with animals leads to animal gods and to polytheism. Consequently, it tended to insist upon the absolute uniqueness of man; and from that it encouraged the notion that all other living creatures exist only to serve man's needs.»[66] For the farmer who keeps a consecrated picture of Antonius in his pigsty, livestock represents not only his entire worldly wealth and his livelihood, but also a relationship closely intertwined with his life. His animals are prone to accident and disease and need the protection of a saint, as much as he does himself. On some small mountain farms, which are not highly mechanised, there is still today a natural relationship with animals, which has been lost on many modern farms. This is why in Switzerland, especially in Catholic mountain areas, January 17, St. Antonius Day, remains an important date in the farming calendar.

Antonius is the patron saint of cattle, cattle breeding and agriculture generally in other countries as well. In Italy and Spain, but also in certain places in Switzerland, he is also the patron saint of pets, including dogs, cats, chickens and horses. Even today, in many places in Europe, these creatures are blessed in front of the church on January 17. In former times, bread and salt for the cattle were consecrated on that day. In France, the oats for the cattle, pigs and chickens were even blessed during Mass itself. Antonius was expected, above all, to provide protection against livestock disease. In Switzerland, in Antonius week, which is usually the third week in January, pilgrimages were made to the Emauskapelle in Bremgarten to pray for protection against misfortune in the cowshed, and especially in the pigsty. St. Antonius is still venerated there.

We see that in connection with the Antonius cult, the animal became an established feature of ecclesiastical custom, arising from people's needs. As we know, animals were revered as divine creatures in many cultures. We think, for example, of the totem animal of archaic man and of many gods in the great religions presented wholly or partly as animals.[67]

What is the origin of this veneration of animals from which we have so distanced ourselves today? Not only do animals have better faculties of perception, such as hearing, sight, smell and an uncanny sense of direction, they are also faster and stronger, have greater stamina than humans and

66 J. Krutch, *The World of Animals,* p. 21f.

67 R. Abt-Baechi, *Animals and Animal Dreams,* p. 19.

Fig. 19: Blessing of the sheep. Mallorca.

are often better adapted to their habitat. In archaic cultures, animals were thus always admired, respected and revered. Today the divine aspect of the relationship with animals has disappeared, their last remaining secrets having apparently been dispelled by the natural sciences. And yet we never cease to be amazed by the fact that animals seem to have a kind of absolute knowledge about how to behave in a way that befits their nature. They live, survive, kill and die in complete accordance with the laws of nature. In Jung's words: «In certain respects the animal is superior to man. It has not yet blundered into consciousness nor pitted a self-willed ego against the power from which it lives; on the contrary, it fulfils the will that actuates it in a well-nigh perfect manner. Were it conscious, it would be morally better than man.»[68]

In folk tales from around the world, animals have supernatural or divine powers. M.-L. von Franz, who was able to draw on the knowledge of several hundred fairy tales, has never found any exception to the rule that the winner is always the one who earns the thanks and help of animals.[69]

68 C. G. Jung, *The Archetypes and the Collective Unconscious* [CW 9/I], § 420.

69 M.-L. von Franz, "The problem of Evil in Fairytales", In: *Archetypal Dimensions of the Psyche*, p. 89.

Fig. 20: Animal Blessing in front of the Laurentius church in Wuppertal (DE).

The symbolism of these tales expresses clearly the fact that it is always the animal instinct or the animal soul of man that is helpful. Depending on what animal it is, we can see which instinctive aspect of human nature is symbolised. In fairy tales, the animals help the hero to win the hand of the princess and to replace the old king, or to ensure the princess is saved by the right suitor. The tales usually end with successful renewal or replacement, a final and complete equilibrium, which corresponds to our psychological goal of inner wholeness. It is precisely because animals will do only what corresponds to the set pattern of their lives that they themselves also often become a symbol of this inner wholeness in the dreams of modern man.[70] They teach people to find themselves, so to speak, to fulfil their human destiny, their individuation.

Many saints are reported to have been on friendly terms with animals. It may have been assumed that they had gained the trust of the animals by their kindness and gentleness. However, the reason why this relationship is presumably so exemplary is that the saints had overcome their own animal nature through their pious way of life. Their animal nature presented them with exceptionally serious problems, as we have seen in

70 Cf. R. Abt-Baechi, *Animals and Animal Dreams.*

the chapter on devils, precisely because of their ascetic life of abstention. Indeed, the animals first appeared as terrible demons to Antonius, but this changed with the passage of time. Thus instead of with demons, Antonius was depicted with a harmless pig in the medieval pictures of the West. The overcoming of the animal nature actually turned into a connection to the animal nature.

Of all animals, the one to which Antonius is closest is the pig, whose patron saint he is. The pig can be found on almost all of his images, where, being a traditional feature of his cult, it occupies the most space. Similarly the names he is given usually include the pig. In Italy, for instance, he is known as 'Antonio del Porco'. In Estonia, Antonius was even referred to as the pig-god![71] He was also the patron saint of swineherds, butchers and brushmakers. For Christmas, New Year's Eve and on Antonius' Day, pigs were slaughtered, the meat was taken to church to be consecrated or sacrificed on the Saint's altar, and then pieces of the meat were distributed among the poor. We also know that the monks of the Antonite monastery were great pig breeders, and their pigs, wearing a bell, were allowed to move around freely. In Switzerland, these pigs were often looked after by the local parishes. This custom has been put forward as an explanation for the relationship between Antonius and the pig, but the wealth of non-Christian tradition woven around the pig and connecting it with the Antonius cult, suggests a broader significance, and we shall now look into this more closely.

The pig no longer has many positive associations for us except in the expression 'the lucky piglet', the piggy bank and the New Year's piglet. Our New Year's Eve lucky piglet has its roots in northern European customs dating back to pre-Christian times, with the Yule boar or the Yule pig, which was originally sacrificed at Christmas time (Yule). In later times, a roasted piglet or a cake in the form of a pig was placed on the table until the New Year. Then, it was distributed partly amongst the family members and animals, or just among the animals in the house, and partly mixed with the seedlings for the New Year. In many places, farm labourers and horses or oxen received some at sowing time so that the new crop would do well. In Frazer's *The Golden Bough* many more examples can be

71 For the Pig see H. Bächtold-Stäubli, *Handwörterbuch des deutschen Aberglaubens,* vol. II, 1469-1509, "Schwein".

Fig. 21: Antonius pig. Wall painting. In the church of St. Matthäus in Murau (DE).

found.[72] Wherever one went, the pig was associated with agriculture and played a prominent role in harvesting customs and traditions, in which it is a symbol of growth and fertility.

For farmers, the pig signified wealth, a blessing of nature. A rich harvest was also always regarded in those earlier times as a gift from the great Mother Nature. This is why the customs surrounding the Nature or Corn Mother were found alongside those associated with the pig. For example, all over Europe, the Corn Mother was commonly believed to be sitting inside the last sheaf of corn, which is why it was often referred to as the sow.[73]

On the strength of its connection with Mother Nature, the pig was commonly held to have superior knowledge, especially in matters concerning a future marriage partner, number of children, birth and so on. If a pregnant woman were to kick a pig, for example, it was believed that she would have a difficult birth. The pig is here virtually equated with Mother Nature. In its relationship with Mother Nature, the pig also

72 Cf. J. G. Frazer, *The Golden Bough.*

73 Ibid.

plays an important role in mythology. The great Nordic Mother Goddess *Freja* is called *syr,* meaning 'pig' and she rides a pig with the name of *Gullinbursti Hildisvini*, 'Gold Bristly Battle Boar.[74] *Demeter*, the Greek fertility and corn mother goddess, is not only depicted as a pig, but was originally probably venerated as a pig. At the autumn festivals, pork was eaten in her honour, and it was also mixed with seedlings. The Egyptian sky goddess, *Nut*, is represented as a sow suckling her young, so she also embodies life-creating, maternal fertility. The pig in Ancient Egypt thus became a good luck sign, but at the same time, it was considered unclean. Pigs were not allowed in the vicinity of temples, and anyone who came into contact with one, had to bathe immediately. Swineherds were banned from entering sanctuaries or shrines. Eating pork was frowned upon, although in cult sacrifice it was considered to be sacred food. This is probably due to the fact that the pig is also associated with the dark, dangerous side of Mother Nature, and thus also with grim and terrible death, eat or be eaten. Pigs and some other animals are actually capable of eating their own young immediately after birth. Jung says that the animal mother instinct is very close to a terrible form of destructiveness. That is why archaic mother goddesses such as the Indian *Kali* or the Greek *Artemis of Ephesus* and some primitive mother figures of archaic tribes, have something grotesquely cruel about them, often even obscene as well, or at least something so remote from our world that we have difficulty in empathising with it.[75] In Greek mythology, we find the dangerous aspect of the mother archetype in the sorceress *Circe*, who, as aforementioned, turned *Odysseus* and his companions into pigs. We need to bear this destructive side in mind when we speak here of the pig mainly as an embodiment of positive maternal femininity.

The gift of prophecy meant that the pig, with some other creatures in Western folklore, came to be regarded as an oracle animal, to which people turned for help in seeing into the future. The original reason for this was probably the fact that animals often seem to hear, see and sense more than humans do. In myth and legend, because of their closeness to the destiny-determining Nature Mother, animals have themselves become authorities

74 A.v. Ström/H. Biezais, *Germanische und baltische Religion,* p. 152.

75 [10] C. G. Jung, *Visions II,* p. 956.

in this sphere. As we shall see later – and many instances of this have been recorded – the connection to this aspect of the mother archetype also gives the pig the ability to detect, unearth and watch over treasure, to track down the sunken bells of legendary fame and to guard hidden springs. If they are left alone, pigs are almost always rooting around in the earth!

The pig, viewed symbolically, is a fertile aspect of the inner realm of Mother Earth, the unconscious psyche, capable of creative renewal. It shares this general symbolism, of course, with all animals, since the germs of the new are always to be found in the unconscious area of instinct. Animals often appear in dreams pointing to this capacity for psychological renewal. The pig, as a domestic animal, with the corresponding typical characteristics, is especially close to people, which means to consciousness. This makes it a very helpful symbol, because it is able to connect the internal and external features of human nature in a fruitful and positive way. This connection apparently has a lasting effect on the development of both our inner and our outer life.

We can thus say that in its closeness to the feminine-maternal forces of destiny, the pig represents a side of us which instinctively senses where the path of life will take us and what fate has in store for us, especially with regard to psychological growth and renewal. In a seminar, M.-L. von Franz once described the analyst as a 'truffle pig', whose task is to 'sniff out' and dig up the new possibilities opened up to the analysand, in the fertile potential and hidden treasures of the unconscious!

According to popular belief, the pig is also competent for all possible forms of magic, whether it be for luck, fertility, love, protection or defence. The nature mother is the great sorceress, and what she creates was always regarded as a miracle. Today, modern science strives to dispel the mystery behind all the miracles of nature, and yet we still speak casually of 'enchanted nature' if we are impressed by her beauty. The same is true of inner nature, which produces our 'magical' dreams. When we dream, we are in the midst of an unknown world in which everything, every transformation, everything apparently impossible, is possible. Dreams may leave us feeling impressed, happy, exalted, sullen, or even shattered. In the past, wherever people were influenced, controlled, or affected by the contents of the unconscious, magic was usually the only explanation.

Medicine men and sorcerers of archaic peoples owed their power to their special skill in being able to establish contact with these unconscious forces.

The magic associated with the pig was especially concerned with human relationships, with the fascination and feeling of eros, arising from an unconscious, instinctual dynamic. There is often something irrational about relationships between people, something that is beyond conscious control. Whether or not a connection is formed and whether or not it continues, often seems to depend on the arbitrary forces of destiny. And sometimes it is a pig that is responsible for the bond that forms between people! Of course, this is not always positive, because any 'enchantment' automatically entails loss of ego consciousness, or even possession by an archetype. It includes overwhelming sexual attraction, which can 'cast a spell' on men and women, blinding them to all reason.

In folk medicine, the pig has a very positive significance, and not just the pig itself, but almost everything that is related to it, such as stall, straw, food trough, is also considered to have medicinal benefits. This is probably because a sow with her many piglets and at least as many generously filled teats, is a fitting image for a rich, instinctive, motherly feeling and a warm physicality. As long as this motherly love is not restricting and oppressive (as every farmer knows, piglets are always in danger of being crushed), a young child can leave the secure orbit of its mother behind and take its first steps into the world beyond, and is itself later capable of that instinctive warmth, that nourishing, healing eros, which is the foundation of the ability to form relationships.

These maternal aspects of the image of Antonius with the pig can make sense also to a modern woman. In everything relating to pregnancy, birth and child-rearing, today's woman often has access to little guidance, traditional or otherwise, which she can take for granted and follow calmly. Modern so-called 'mobile television-grandmothers' rarely have any useful experience-based knowledge to pass on to their daughters. Young women today often resort to books as a source of guidance, which can be helpful, but it sometimes causes more confusion than clarity. It can also lead to the temptation to do things in a rational and too masculine way, rather than with the necessary instinct and feeling. There is the risk then that a woman may lapse into a sterile, cold and uncaring animus attitude. This would be an example of the pig's vulnerability to the Devil, a subject we shall return

Fig. 22: Sow with piglet.

to later. Labouring under the delusion and conviction that there is only one correct way to behave, such mothers can be incredibly vicious with their children, without even realising it. However, where a woman can connect with the positive 'feeling of pigs', this is instinctively understood by the child, being itself largely an instinctual creature. It is precisely in connection with children that the relationship to animals can really help a modern mother regain her own lost instinctive reactions, with all their attendant energy, as long as she is not afraid to follow her feelings, even where they don't appear in an appropriate form. Like an annoyed animal mother she may sometimes feel she needs to take a swipe at her child with her paw. Though what modern mother wishes to be regarded as uncaring? The dark side of the archetypal nature mother is alien and threatening to her. If she lets herself get carried away, planting a harmless smack on the bottom of her child, she is usually smitten by pangs of conscience, quite apart from the fact that the general consensus today condemns this simple form of discipline as violence against the child.

A difficult task facing modern women in bringing up children, which is not made any easier by the double burden of career and home, is to integrate the light and dark pig aspects of unconscious instinct. How much of this instinctual relationship does she wish to or have to surrender to day-nursery staff, surrogate mothers and state institutions for the sake of her professional life and her own intellectual development? Perhaps it is no coincidence that women today are again increasingly seeking to explore and maintain a relationship with animals. The influx of women into animal-care jobs is enormous, and horse-loving young girls can be found in stables everywhere, seeking warmth and relationships in their love for these animals. Today's women probably suffer more than men from the feeling of being cut off from their 'animal side', even if the modern age provides them with many ways of lightening their load in this sphere. Births can now be planned and the traditional gender roles can be turned upside down. For the first time in the history of mankind, it is possible for women to survive without having to obey their instincts. Whereas in the past they instinctively did the right thing in everyday life, because that was where their strength lay and because there were no alternatives, today they have at their disposal the baby monitor, the so-called electric grandmother, the shopping mall, the Internet and State care. Furthermore, while the computerisation of so much of modern life has made many things easier and has created new opportunities, many people either soon forget the downside of the technology or else they suffer and feel helpless. The more women adapt – or are forced to adapt – to a more efficient and convenient way of life, the greater the risk they run of being cut off from their instinctive feminine vitality. Of course, we cannot turn back the clock and have women washing on the riverbank again and mothering eighteen children. There does, however, seem to be a deeply felt need among modern women for a reconnection to their unconscious, instinctive energy. The more individual women begin to respond to the call of their own true nature and find ways to accommodate it within the context of their modern lives, the more we might begin to see a real shift in the general cultural attitude towards the whole sphere of instinctive life.

Where a feminine nature deity, such as the Greek Demeter, is worshipped in a culture in which all areas of feminine life are included, this feminine life is in itself meaningful, and indeed, in the figure of the goddess, is the object of general veneration. In our Christian culture, in which the Virgin Mary embodies only the light characteristics of the feminine deity, there is no divine role model for dealing with the issues of sexuality, eros, and female concerns including the nurturing of family and relationships, birth, maternity and child-rearing, i.e. the very areas where there needs to be a connection to nature and instinct. This absence of a divine role model is one of the underlying reasons why the traditional feminine life has sunk so low in general esteem that many women feel they would just as soon take on any other 'job'. Indeed, there is considerable social pressure in this direction and many women willingly 'surrender'. Feminine life, which includes family and children as a central value, is commonly perceived as unimportant, old fashioned, conservative, meaningless. Life in a soulless block of flats does not help to improve the situation. Therefore, if a woman has to – or has chosen to – devote herself completely to family and children, she may well feel a vague sense of inferiority in relation to the masculine working world, and that is not just because she is not contributing financially to the family. The woman will often try to fit back into the working world as soon as possible, usually taking on additional burdens. On the other hand, many women want to work and carve out a career for themselves as a matter of choice and not only for financial reasons; they want a mental challenge, a position of leadership and responsibility, or involvement in politics, and they seek to establish their credentials in the male world. However, this choice usually entails a degree of conflict with the instinctual side of a woman's nature. This instinctual side has to do with her forming relationships and with her meeting her physical needs to achieve a 'pig-like' sense of well-being. It might mean her allowing herself, at times, to be as lazy as a pig in its wallow. However, it also means her being connected to her natural libido, energy, unconscious drive and life force, which are all part of animal instinct. Wherever the pig instinct is repressed, leading a shadowy existence in the unconscious, or worse, where it is abused and tormented, the woman suffers from a neurotic split. It is akin to keeping an animal under conditions that are over-crowded, cruel and inappropriate to the species! In the psyche, the neglect or maltreatment of instinct causes a loss of vitality and energy, which may manifest in bouts of depression or anxiety, and it is not uncommon for otherwise inexplicable physical symptoms to appear. This, of course, also applies to the feminine side of a man, even if with a man it seems to take longer before the problem cannot be ignored.

In the working world of today, it is above all the hectic pace that is harmful to the pig side of the psyche. Pigs are easily frightened and cannot tolerate aimless running around and erratic behaviour. So it is not easy to give the inner pig freedom, on the one hand, and yet, on the other, to protect it against restlessness and pointless bustling about. We also have to keep an eye on its negative sides: dirt, laziness, gluttony, oppressive maternal pressure, compulsive sexual desire, fears, chaotic emotionality and impulsiveness. That is what too much of the pig would mean! But, as we have seen, too little of the pig means a lack of maternal eros, even for one's own 'inner' children, i.e. one's own potential, and it means neglect of the physical body and a general lack of human warmth. So we somehow have to find a middle ground in our relationship to the inner pig.

In accordance with all the above amplifications of the pig, Antonius, the ascetic desert saint, acquires a distinctly feminine quality, with which he seems to be perfectly at ease in all the pictures. Popular sentiment apparently resolved early on that male Christian asceticism and the purely spiritual striving for perfection could not really do justice to human nature. For dealing with imperfect, inner nature is what ultimately determines whether the instincts, the internal animals, become helpers or malicious demons. With a man, the instinctive realm belongs to the anima, which often appears in mythological stories, legends, fairy tales and dreams, as an animal. We recall that the anima personifies the unconscious, female side of a man, which initially he usually projects onto a real woman. The anima embodies «vague feelings and moods, prophetic hunches, receptiveness to the irrational, capacity for personal love, feeling for nature, and – last but not least – his relation to the unconscious». If a man experiences the anima as negative, she appears as irritable, depressed moods, uncertainty, insecurity and touchiness. «These anima moods cause a sort of dullness, a fear of disease, of impotence, or of accidents. The whole of life takes on a sad an oppressive aspect. Such dark moods can even lure a man to suicide, in which case the anima becomes a death demon.» According to the circumstances, she can become a soul guide or a dangerous seductress.[76]

76 M.-L. von Franz, "The Anima: The woman within". In: C. G. Jung, *Man and his Symbols,* p. 177.

Fig. 23: Temptation of Saint Antonius. Niklaus Manuel Deutsch. 1517/18.

The anima generally can weaken the character of a man and make him non-conformist, moody, jealous and vain. If she is a 'pig-anima', she can, for example, bring up erotic fantasies, or produce very unconscious or compulsive sexuality and sensuality. On a deep, unconscious level, the pig can also mean a strong attachment to the mother. Such a mother complex can have the effect of making a man expect a lot from life – he expects life to be a nourishing mother pig. Whereas missing confidence in the pig can give rise in a man to a feeling of constant inadequacy, fear and an inability to assert himself and his own needs in relation to the female sex. So here again, we have first too much pig, then too little! Both situations disrupt the flow of life and the balance of psychological opposites, outer and inner, conscious and unconscious life.

Where there is too much 'pigness', in the psyche of either a man or a woman, some of it would need to be sacrificed. The idea of sacrificing what we have described as negative pig behaviour might seem easy to understand. But it is actually not so simple, because the pig has a special significance as a sacrificial animal. Behind every sacrificial act, deemed at all times by mankind as necessary and useful, there is ultimately the idea of renewal of life, bringing fertility and new possibilities, a new step in the development of consciousness and of culture. We saw earlier that according to popular belief, the pig is closely associated with harvest customs, maternal deities and fertility demons. Pigs are sacrificed most commonly at harvest time when the blessing of nature is performed. This close connection of the pig to the archetype of Mother Nature is of great psychological significance. It imbues instinctive mother love with a power that extends far beyond the personal, which explains why the rite of sacrifice makes sense symbolically. The instinctive connection of the mother to the child has to be sacrificed step-by-step so that the child can develop its individual character and is not prevented by too much mother love from living its own life. Probably one of the most difficult tasks a mother has to face is not just to let go of her child but also to encourage it to develop in its own way. Bringing up a child thus always involves time and again a sacrifice of unconscious maternal power claims on the child. Mothers who identify with the positive side of the archetype of the great nature and animal mother often have, – notwithstanding all appearances to the contrary, a destructive effect on those around them. It is common knowledge that excessive love and mothering is actually a claim to power and is nothing more than possession by the archetype of the Great Mother. It is very difficult for a woman to identify the destructive aspects of the mother archetype operating through her, since they are not part of her conscious personality. The question is then how far her own sense of responsibility extends, and what simply happens through her without her actual intervention. For a woman this can lead to great uncertainty with regard to her maternal role. Sometimes it is only with the help of her dreams that she can begin to distinguish between her ego and the archetype, between what she is as a mother and what the archetype of the great mother produces in her.

According to popular belief, pigs are sometimes ridden by witches and devils. The positive pig-aspects of the mother goddess, which include eros and feeling connections, seem to be easily jeopardised by something destructive that intervenes in this sphere from the unconscious background of the psyche. Popular belief also has it that the pig is highly susceptible to witchcraft and the evil eye. How are we to understand these beliefs in psychological terms?

Pigs are very people-friendly and intelligent. If they are granted sufficient freedom, they can be as good as dogs in relating to people. It is fairly obvious that this characteristic of relatedness within the psyche can easily be destroyed by power-obsessed evil claims to power. Then the pig instinct becomes destructive. It can, for example, then embody a primitive sexuality and sensuality, devoid of all feeling, and having more to do with selfishness and the wish to dominate than with love, with obsession instead of relationship. Viewed psychologically, this transformation of the pig side is usually brought about by a destructive animus or a power-obsessed feminine side. A man's anima is also capable of becoming a witch! She can sometimes introduce something poisonous or even dishonest into a relationship, which is difficult to grasp, because, as far as possible, it steers clear of any direct confrontation. She will not be caught! Similarly, when a woman has been hurt in her love life, or feels that she is not being taken seriously as a woman, the animus can impose on her a cold, rigid attitude, which she may find difficult to shake off alone. She becomes possessive and self-opinionated, acting only according to her principles, which can destroy her relationships and undermine her femininity. The pig, with its warm and instinctual feeling relationship, is then ridden by the Devil, and transformed into something destructive.

A case in point is when two people involved in an argument fail to understand why – despite all their sincere efforts to communicate, to explain their point of view, to reach out to each other – they cannot settle the dispute sensibly. Instead they just continue to offend each other. The result is that warm and friendly feelings are often exposed to the cold blast of provocative argument, mutual recriminations or unreasonable assertions. A greater awareness here that attention must be paid to the positive and nurturing aspect of natural, instinctive feeling, symbolised in the pig, could bring about a less abrasive attitude. Sometimes it can be helpful to the pig if the argument is combined with good food and a glass of wine!

We must now move away from the pig, and examine the fact that, through the *corn mother disease*, Antonius is also connected with the dark, even malicious, side of the mother archetype. He is venerated as the healer of this illness. In popular belief, the Corn Mother appears in her role as a witch who captures small children and causes the corn to wither. Moreover, she is a goddess of disease, because she is responsible for the highly toxic so-called corn mother disease that lurks hidden in the harvest. According to popular belief, Antonius himself, the great healer of this terrible plague-like disease, is also the bringer of the disease. He shares this un-Christian characteristic with the plague demons of legends, but also with plague Saints Rochus and Sebastian. Thus contrary to the purely male image of the pious ascetics of the desert, the Christian saint appears in medieval representations connected with the archetype of the Great Mother, which contains all the contradictions of nature. Antonius becomes less Christian, but maybe a little more human.

The corn mother disease or the Antonius fire (*feu infernal*, *ignis sacer*), raged throughout Europe in the Middle Ages, from Sweden to Spain, from France to Russia. This epidemic was caused by people eating bread made from rye or other grains infected with ergot fungi. Alkaloids in the fungi produced the symptoms of ergotism, a fiery reddening of the skin, fever, cold feelings in the joints, vomiting, delirium and hallucinations of fire flames, attacks by wild animals and so on. The condition was often confused with syphilis. In Mexico, the poisonous ergot was traditionally used as a drug and apparently it is still used to produce hallucinogenic effects. In the 1930s, ergot, the toxin of the mother corn, entailed the discovery of LSD and its hallucination effect. So it was also used therapeutically in psychiatry. In classical Greece, Hippocrates described the stimulating effect of the corn mother poison during birth. Ergot causes uterine contractions, so it can be used to induce abortions and to stop maternal bleeding after childbirth. It still has a place in modern obstetric practice. Ergot also has other uses today in general internal medicine and in geriatrics. Here once again we have the destructive and yet healing aspect of the maternal.

So highly dangerous poison can be found in grain, of all things, a basic staple of life. The fact that this poison and the disease it caused could be explained by the effect of an otherwise positive, food-providing mother goddess, corresponds to the ambivalence of the unconscious psyche, which can be the source of thoughts and impulses that are toxic and destructive, yet also creative, renewing and healing. Mixed with the motherliness of a not very conscious woman, there may, for example, be tiny doses of an invisible, unconscious poison – perhaps in the form of negative thoughts about people and the world generally – which infiltrates the whole atmosphere around her. Incredible as it may seem, a genuinely caring and nurturing mother can have a destructive effect on her children, through this insidious poison, even weakening their will to live, for children are the ones most exposed to the unconscious influences of the mother. Psychological poison can be produced when our mental or emotional needs are not met. Sibylle Birkhäuser in *The Mother – Archetypal Image in Fairy Tales,* says: «Among women, the ones who have a poisonous influence on other people are particularly those who have failed to achieve some important aim in their lives. For example, if a woman has not developed her mind although she could have done so, and has thus betrayed the process of coming to consciousness in herself, her positive maternal instincts change over the course of time into a corrosive influence on her family and others.»[77]

Contents of the unconscious that are poisonous, and that can even make a person ill, also manifest as unbearable compulsion and infantile demands, irritated reactions, unacceptable thoughts, fantasies etc.

77 S. Birkhäuser-Oeri, by *The Mother - Archetypal Image in Fairy Tales,* p. 107.

Fig. 24: St. Antonius. Workshop Hans Geiler, 1520.

The less we are aware of them, the more they can poison our lives and our relationships. Unfortunately we cannot really cause them to disappear through conscious effort or will-power, or have them explained away by someone who means well. Intellectual insight alone does not bring about a real change of attitude. Indeed, with the intellect, we tend to fend off the painful and depressing feelings of inferiority that come with facing the unpleasant sides of the unconscious shadow and, in this way, we protect ourselves against too much venom. For, actually, we can only take the shadow in limited doses, when it crops up in painful ways in our lives. Dreams also bring up the toxic aspects of the shadow, but dreams are very helpful because they always seem to deliver just as much 'poison' as the ego consciousness can cope with at any one moment. In the right doses, the suffering associated with taking responsibility for the poison can be borne, without the shadow problem having to be projected again onto other people or situations. Then the poison can turn into medicine and can have a healing effect on inner and outer life. This can be compared with the healing effect of mother corn poison. If consciousness cooperates, the unconscious, from which the destructive substance emerges, can also bring healing.

Animus and anima, in their undifferentiated, shadowy forms, can also give rise to 'toxic' inappropriate or harmful reactions and behaviour, and to poisonous thoughts and fantasies. Dealing with such unpleasant shadow material can set in motion a development of consciousness and a process of healing that would not be possible without it. That is why the most difficult people in analysis are those who seemingly have no problems! The negative moods or erotic fantasies of the anima, however, can, if taken seriously, develop into positive, creative life incentives. Similarly, the stubbornly held views, willful self-righteousness, wishful thinking, and feelings of inferiority that the animus initially produces in a woman can, if caught, then deliberately and consciously suffered, eventually bring a broadening of her horizons and the development of initiative, mental clarity, insight and creativity.

On the one hand, there are dark, even extremely dangerous aspects of the mother goddess or the unconscious, which can, on the other hand, bring about healing and new life. Everywhere we encounter this ambivalence of unconscious contents. Each dream image must therefore be examined carefully, because it can always have a destructive as well as an uplifting aspect. Whether, in a particular case, it is able to shed light on the current situation, and how much of it can or must be integrated, can only be clarified, first, by careful study of the case history, and then by pondering the symbolic statements of the dream image. It is therefore not surprising, these days, when it is so easy just to swallow a pill for any ailment, that many people are reluctant to adopt a remedy that requires so much effort on their part. It takes courage to surrender to this ambivalent remedy, and a strong and diligent consciousness to deal with it! For there is no guarantee that it will not call into question all one's current views and one's lifestyle. Typically, such an in-depth 'healing process' needs the help of a 'midwife', i.e. a skilled person who can bring to the situation a knowledge of the symbolic language of the unconscious.

If we take one more look at the significance of the pig in folklore, what strikes us is that it has a close relationship to the otherworldly or the spiritual sphere. In legends and folk tales, the pig often appears as a ghostly creature, a nocturnal spectre that is alarming or threatening to humans and animals. Legends recount how one can be marked for life or even die after an encounter with such a ghost.[78] The pig is also connected to the accursed souls of the dead that have to continue to exist in a ghostly form. In this capacity, the pig belongs to the death mother, to the realm of the dead or the night side. In psychological terms, this can be understood as meaning that the unconscious side – where things lurk in wait for us in the dark – is haunted by the broken off and unredeemed parts of the soul.

Sagas and legends often deal with the sexuality and sensuality so condemned by the Church and, appearing then in the projection onto such a ghost pig. It means that someone had committed that sin a long time ago and is now doomed to wander around in this form. Redemption is rare and it is always a frightening experience for those who meet the ghost animal. Sometimes things emerge from our unconscious that seem so strange to us as ghost animals. If we go back to study our family history, we sometimes discover that our own difficulties have their roots in the unresolved problems of our ancestors. The potential not realised in their lives roams around in our unconscious, so to speak, and we have to drag it

78 A.Büchli, *Mythologische Landeskunde von Graubünden,* I, 197f., II, 354 and 412 f. and others.

out into the light of consciousness and examine it in order to "redeem the dead souls". This, roughly speaking, is the meaning of many ghost stories and tales of redemption.[79] When 'soul parts' appear to us in dreams, we can perhaps see what role they play in our lives. Our whole confrontation with the symbol of the pig is an example of dragging a soul animal out into the light!

In official ecclesiastical Christianity, the pig aspect of the psyche has, as we have seen, been placed largely on the side of evil. The Valais mountain peasant woman and midwife, Marie Métrailler, describes very vividly the extent of her suffering as a child at the mercy of a fearsome Church which condemned as sinful any remark related to the instinctual side of life, any expression of joie de vivre, vitality, love and especially sexuality. Even the most innocent child was threatened by grisly details of terrible punishments in Hell.[80] With this attitude from the Church, a significant part of natural unconscious functioning was suppressed, and with it a source of life, growth and renewal.

The pig as an attribute of a saint complements the Christian ascetic view, offering a revaluation of man's instinctual side. The pig is now transferred back to where it comes from, namely, from the vicinity of the divine, in other words, the unconscious. Granted, nowadays, we may have shrugged off the shackles of sin threateningly imposed upon us by the Church and we may have made the sphere of eros, love and sexuality more accessible in our lives. Indeed, everything in this sphere now seems possible; trivialisation and commercialisation know no bounds. However, having said that, because the pig aspects of life are rooted in the natural mother, which means in the unconscious, this instinctual side of life ultimately eludes us. Unless we are aware of this problem, we can be affected without realising it, cast under a spell and robbed of our freedom of choice. *Mater Materia* retaliates by transforming pigs into devils and witch animals, as we have learned from the sagas. Thus, at the core of our apparently free modern life, there may be greed, gluttony, unrestrained materialism, addiction to pleasure, and childish dependence on the social institutions that become our surrogate mothers.

79 G. Isler, *Lumen Naturae. Zum religiösen Sinn von Alpensagen.* And: A. Büchli, *Mythologische Landeskunde von Graubünden,* III, 711.

80 M.-M.Brumagne (Ed.), *Die Reise der Seele. Die Lebensgeschichte der Marie Métrailler.*

So the symbol of the pig expresses psychological characteristics which are still of importance for us today. These are 'soul parts' of an animal-instinctual nature which, under the influence of Christianity, have largely disappeared from our field of consciousness. As we have seen, these aspects of human nature have been excluded in the dogmatic figure of Mary, the Christian image of the divine mother. The whole area of sexuality and the body, symbolised in the pig, was an important part of pagan cults of the great mother goddess. In Christian times, it was attributed to Eve, the temptress who brought sin and death. By way of contrast, according to Christian concepts, it was through Mary that the light «which drove away the darkness brought by Eve»[81] was created. This separation of Eve and Mary led to the two aspects of the archetypal mother figure, the light and the dark, being torn asunder.

In alchemy, however, Eve was still a unifying figure, being very much the primeval mother of all living things, as well as the one who brought about the expulsion from Paradise, which led to death.[82] Alchemy experienced its heyday just when the Antonius cult was at its height. It dealt with the rediscovery of nature, the body and the problem of *materia*. This recognition of the feminine principle seemed a promising cultural development at the time. A similarly hopeful trend in the Middle Ages was the cult of courtly love between a Christian knight and his lady, which brought a new kind of relatedness between man and woman. Also known as the *Minnedienst*, this brief flowering of the eros principle did not survive the Reformation nor the increasing prevalence of extraversion that followed the Renaissance.[83] For the more simple-minded people of the period, the pig of Antonius expressed in symbolic form the same neglected aspects of life that preoccupied the alchemists. Thus, like the symbolic images of alchemy, it compensated a one-sided view of the human psyche.

According to M.-L. von Franz, with the rapidly growing veneration of the Virgin Mary after the period of courtly love, the image of the feminine within the Church gained in importance, but «with great mental

81 M.-L. von Franz speaks about the historical development of the conception of the figures of Eve and Maria in: *Aurora Consurgens,* p. 245. (In: C .G. Jung [CW 14], Edition 1957).

82 Ibid., p. 245.

83 M.-L. von Franz, *The Feminine in Fairytales,* p. 139.

reservations and precautions for disinfection of her dark aspect. [...] The dark aspect of the antique mother goddess has not yet reappeared in our civilisation, which must leave a question mark in our minds, because naturally something is lacking.»[84] The pig is a case in point. Maybe that is why it is still difficult for women to present to the outside world their own real needs and to assert themselves without 'animosity' (the aggression of the animus). Very often it is the animus that is responsible for women not sensing what is actually theirs by right and what is not. In this regard it can be helpful for women to take time to think things over, to apply 'common sense', to listen to their own feelings even when they may not seem to be appropriate; to give the pig room. Dreams often clearly point in the same direction.

For many men, it is equally difficult to give consideration to their feminine side, for it would bring an irrational feeling element into in their worldview and their external lives. This disturbing element would connect a man with the ambiguities and subtleties of relationship, which are so much at odds with the clear, rational, purposeful approach to life generally more familiar to a man. Unfortunately, the anima side often turns up uninvited and in an unpleasant form, such as an incredibly bad mood, and she makes a man feel insecure, sorry for himself and perhaps permanently guilty. Self-pity can quickly turn into anger and aggression. Then the man lapses into an emotional state, overwhelmed by the witch-pig. If he could sacrifice it, he would give his feelings the opportunity to sense instinctively how to deal with the situation. But mostly, he will try to solve the problem by thinking his way through it, a procedure doomed to failure.

On the collective level, in Europe today, we see how the political thinking and power ambitions of those who govern mean that less and less heed is taken of the feelings and wishes of the people. Many ordinary folk would like more of a say in the collective decision-making process. They are concerned for the plight of the individual, so easily swallowed up by the masses and increasingly lonely, needing not only to be fed and entertained but with spiritual needs too. The political upper class or the ruling collective consciousness increasingly reacts to this restless stirring of the people with a hardening of attitudes and with panic, not without

84 Ibid., p. 25.

justification. For Mother Nature and her animals seem to be making moves underground and cracks are appearing in the unyielding crust. There is a growing risk of a violent eruption on psychic grounds.

In summary, we can say that the communion of the saint with the pig illustrates the union of the spiritual and the instinctive sides of man. The symbol of the pig incorporates values of the feminine and of an eros from our pre-Christian past, which includes more than pure sexuality. The pig is therefore not only an embodiment of the demonic temptations to which Antonius was subjected, or of 'swinish', unbridled drives. In medieval pictures, it conveys much more, namely, a lost sense of connection between 'above and below'. In Switzerland today, for example, very many people suffer more from the meaninglessness of their lives than from a lack of material goods. As we shall see, in quite a few folk tales it is the pig that finds the sunken bells. These bells were very often directly understood as the voice of God, the *vox Dei,* as we learn from old, traditional bell inscriptions that have been handed down to us. But the voice of God was felt at all times to be that which bestows on human life its highest meaning. This brings us to the symbol of the bell, another of our saint's important attributes

7. The Bell

In the dream that was our starting point, the church bells of my home village featured very prominently. The bells suddenly rang out, making a sound that was both chaotic and lacking in harmony, with the result that people walked out of the church. Therefore the main aim of our examination of the bell will be to enlighten the dream content, which is so closely linked with the figure of Antonius in the second part of the dream. To help us understand this dream image, we have already begun to investigate the deeper meaning behind his portraits and his characteristic attributes.

In his pictures, St. Antonius is often seen carrying a bell, either in his hand or on a pole. Sometimes it can be found round the neck of the pig. Generally, a bell was used to ward off demons. For the Antonites, however, it was a special sign, enabling themselves and their pigs to be recognised from afar. Once we regard the bell as a symbol, many more associations emerge. In the past, such a symbol would have been understood as a matter of course, but today some sort of interpretation is called for. By adopting the method of so-called 'amplification', which we have already applied in the previous chapters, we can enrich the symbol, so to speak, with similar or related motifs from folklore, myths, legends and so on, encircling it until some kind of common link suggests itself from the many different facets. In this way we can develop a psychological interpretation in contemporary language, which can connect modern people with their own experiences and, at the same time, with the energy of the archetypal psyche.

The bell as a symbol has a rich background of cultural history and plays a very important role in popular beliefs and tradition.[85] According to the dictionary of German superstitions, no other cult object is so bound up with the emotional life and the imagination of the people as the bell: folk tradition thrives here, rich and multiform, more so than almost

85 About the Bell, cf. the comprehensive collection of P. Sartori, *Das Buch von deutschen Glocken.*

Fig. 25: St. Antonius Eremita, at 1500.

anywhere else.[86] The original significance of the bell was probably in its role in keeping ghosts at bay. It was said to be able to drive away devils, giants and dwarves, wizards and witches, vermin and wild animals, but also exorcise the demons of those possessed or bewitched. Bells were said to break the spell cast on a woman abducted from the human world and, reinforced by the noise of a parade, were driving away the demons who were the enemies of fertility. Bell amulets to protect against evil spirits are also commonly found in the Middle East, as well as in Africa and China. Our cattle bells also originally had this protective function.

On the other hand, while the bells were ringing, evil spirits were said to be out and about, witches searching for herbs for their magic potions, and vampires roaming the area around the churchyard. In so far as it could be heard, the sound of bells was believed to fend off thunder, hail and storms, but on the other hand, it could actually attract them and then the bells would have to be silenced. We shall return later to these contradictory characteristics of bells. The bell has always had a special connection to the other world.[87] Although it is man-made, it seems to have a life of its own, appearing to influence the powers of nature that unconsciously govern people's lives. If we look at the symbolism of the bell more closely, we can learn more about what this means psychologically. Where is there an instance of the bell's influence to be found in our psychological household, as it were, and how does it work? For an answer to this question, let us examine more closely the role that it plays in people's minds.

According to folk tradition, the bell is generally well disposed towards humans. Not only the sound but also the very substance of a bell can have beneficial effects. Contact with it, or with metal freshly scraped off it, for example, is said to cure or prevent disease. Thus the so-called Bell ointment has an important place in folk medicine. The chime of a

86 *Handwörterbuch des deutschen Aberglaubens*, vol. III, 868-876.

87 The inscription in the western main tower of the Mainz cathedral tower reads as follows: «*ANNO DOMINI MCCXCVIII VINCULA PETRI OSANNA HEISIN ICH [...] ALLER MAINZER GLOCKIN UBERDON ICH FULMEN QUANDO SONO PLUVIAS COUM GRANDINE PELLO AMO ALBRECH MACHEN MICH* (In the year of our Lord 1298 at the Feast of Peter in chains Aug. 1. Hosanna I cry [...] I drown out all the bells of Mainz , when I ring, I drive away lightning, rain and hail. Albrech made me.)» The bell was melted down. Recorded on the list of historic bells of Mainz Cathedral.

bell is also of great importance in relation to fertility, be it for the fields, livestock or humans.

The bell with which we are most familiar is probably the church bell, which reminds us time and again that there is a dimension of life other than the everyday one. It may be ushering in a weekday or a Sunday; it may be accompanying a wedding procession to church or a dead man on his final journey. In those places where the bell for evening prayer still rings, this other dimension intervenes directly in the working day and calls for contemplation and reflection. Then the mole is said to surface from the depths of the earth to daylight. The bell sound is thus connected with both the darkness under the earth and with heaven. For us, the sound of a bell can conjure up a special feeling, a distant memory, a mood, a 'feeling sound'. In my dream where the bells in the church ring in a chaotic way, this feeling sound is disturbed.

In folk tales, the bell that accompanies people throughout their everyday lives, is closely related to a village community or a region from which it cannot be stolen or sold off. It returns of its own accord, or stops ringing or breaks down in the new location. Sometimes it sinks into the ground or, more frequently, into the water. According to some legends, the dead refuse to be separated from the bells beneath which they were buried.[88] The various parish bells that rang out on certain occasions, often independent of the church bell, were all inextricably connected with village life, indicating when there was baking or washing, for example, or when it was closing time in the taverns. There was a wine bell, a beer bell, a watchman's bell, a citizens' bell, a school bell and a farm bell, at the centre of each farm, regulating the day's timetable. The sound of the bell always signals the moment in time when it is right to do certain things, calling us to adapt to a certain external order, to summon up the energy to do what needs to be done now. In this sense, it has a consciousness-promoting aspect in relation to collective life. It is significant that, in many places, bells are a bone of contention between long-standing residents and newcomers to the village. The newcomers sometimes try to have the church bells silenced and cow bells banned as noise disturbances, while the residents defend their emotional attachment to the bells.

88 P. Satori, *Das Buch von deutschen Glocken,* p. 26, p. 30.

Fig. 26: Cow bells in the Swiss mountains.

So there is a connection between person, soul and place of which he or she is hardly aware in the present age of increased mobility and general rootlessness. We know that early man lived in an archaic connectedness with his surroundings, that he experienced inner visions in external nature. He came up against witches, gnomes and goblins, supernatural animals and demonic and divine figures of all kinds in the phenomena of nature – weather, landslides, floods, wind, fog, storm, darkness, plague and war, in fact in anything that influenced his life in a way he could not ascribe to himself. With increasing development of consciousness, this *participation mystique* (Lévy-Brühl), this unity of inner and outer nature lost more and more ground. It led to a split between inner psychological space and external space. Once there were no more ghosts to be feared in nature, the way was clear for it to be tamed by technology. The ability to control avalanches and correct the courses of rivers, the early warning system, the ever-present lighting and so on, all provide a feeling of security today, behind which the dangers of the inner forces of nature pale into insignificance.

Only rarely do the important or impressive places mentioned in sagas, connected with certain distinctive features or with special experiences, still speak to us. We can exploit, spoil and destroy a landscape, without it ever occurring to us to be afraid of upsetting the local spirits. Yet, oddly enough, today there are landscapes, old buildings, quaint villages, natural ecological niches for animals and plants and so on, that are regarded as worth protecting, meaning that there are some values that should be preserved rather than destroyed. These places have something that appeals to us, something unspoiled and constant that has to do with a longing for security, relationship, permanence, and contact with nature, with a longing that springs from our soul. Something begins to stir within us, a 'feeling tone' which we imagine our ancestors possessed as part of their everyday lives. It is true that we no longer experience the images of the soul as powerfully effective forces in our environment. We have grown psychologically independent of our environment. But at the same time, with this development of our consciousness, there is a risk that the sound of the inner bell fades away, the inner voice which formerly spoke to us through the environment is no longer heard. That would be the sunken lost bells, referred to in the legends, which can still be heard from afar but are very difficult to trace. The problem of 'loss of soul' is not a new one, but today we can no longer afford to ignore it. It runs parallel to the destruction of our natural habitat. Natural space is, however, still psychological space, soul landscape, and should be given due attention. If today a centuries-old tree is felled by the authorities on rational grounds, there might be a storm of protest, with letters written and accusations made by people who regard it as murder and whose feelings are hurt, yet they are generally dismissed as sentimental and emotional. And so on rational grounds, emotional relatedness to our environment is destroyed again and again.

The fact that according to legends, the bell is bound to its location in some mysterious way, could mean that for earlier people, the voice of the other dimension could only be heard in that one place, to which they were bound in life or in death. That would mean, if one may phrase it thus, that it was an expression of a form of regional or even village unconscious of the people living there. We all, in some way or other, still carry within us those people for whom bell and place belonged inseparably together. Although we no longer project psychic contents onto our surroundings

Fig. 27: Baker's Bell, in St. Petri, Soest (Westfalen, DE).

to the same extent, there is still a part of us which is not indifferent to where we live and to the kind of relationship we have to a certain place. Furthermore, we do not know whether, alongside the projection of an inner content onto a place, there is not also an objective reality to the psychic influence of a place, as Jung speculated.[89] The findings of modern physics can provide grounds today for the hypothesis that a specific 'Lebensraum'

89 C. G. Jung, *Letters*, vol. I, Letter to Emil Egli from 15.9.1943.

(the place where we live) has a direct effect on people.[90] If we listen to our feelings, then this seems quite natural. At any rate, so-called recreational areas have a significantly different effect on our mental well-being than the stressful hustle and bustle of a city subway.

The relationship between the collective psyche of a population and its surroundings is becoming increasingly lost today in the wake of general technological progress and mobility, and the sound of the bell is heard less and less. The larger the Earth's population becomes, and the greater the mass migrations of millions of people, the more urgent the problem of rootlessness and the psychological homelessness of whole nations. Many uprooted people do not belong to those fortunate ones who are able to build a new, close relationship to another place, be it on a South Sea island, or in the desert, or even in a foreign city, where the voice of the bell may sound for them again. Generally speaking, we are condemned to permanent mobility by the very nature of our daily work. We therefore probably have no choice but to accept what we might call a *both – and* situation, i.e. we have to try to restore a connection to the inner spiritual side of life, but without losing touch with the place where we live. If we are aware of this, maybe sometime, somewhere – amid the noise and din of modern restlessness – we can allow ourselves a moment of leisure, when the ancestor within us can recover, that same ancestor who covered distances on foot or on horseback, who coped with darkness by resorting to tallow, oil or candle-light, and for whom life proceeded much more slowly and was much more closely bound to home and homeland. Then we usually feel somehow rested and nourished. Recovery is, of course, what today's 'wellness boom' is all about, and nobody can possibly object to that, except perhaps to point out that there is too much emphasis on the physical aspect. Enormous numbers of extraverted leisure activities are supposed to promote physical and psychological recovery, but very often, because people become over-ambitious and geared to performance, they end up physically and mentally exhausted. The sound of the bell, the link to the spiritual, can usually then no longer be discerned. It is true that the old nature gods may manifest again, but in these circumstances in the form of obsessions, seeking daringly spectacular adventures at risk to life and limb, needing to experience total freedom, and so on. What ultimately lies

90 Cf. Th. Abt, *Progress without Loss of Soul*. Part 3, Chapter 5.

behind this kind of drive is probably the unconscious need to re-establish the lost union with the spiritual dimension. Sometimes, this need is only satisfied by a fatal accident.

The ringing of bells used to be closely interwoven not only with the daily routine, but also with the life's customs and traditions in general. It announced births, baptisms, marriages and deaths, each having its own specific ring, so that every inhabitant of the village knew what was meant and could respond accordingly. The tolling of the funeral bell was the one that lasted longest. According to popular belief, only when the funeral bell rang could the soul embark on its journey, and only when accompanied by the ringing of the bell could it finally cross to the other world. The dying bell, which was rung before the actual death, summoned the local people to pray collectively for the person dying. To protect him or her from being attacked by evil spirits or the Devil, small hand bells were also used, which, among other names, were called Antonius bells.[91] Bells were also believed to announce imminent death by a special sound, or by concurrence with special external events or by a mysterious, independent ring.

The bell reminds people again and again about what stands behind things. It causes an emotional reaction, or an emotional prelude to another, a numinous area that is related to the all-important, what happens to him. Birth, baptism, marriage and death represent transitions into a new stage of human existence in the traditional community, and bell-ringing is a part of the accompanying rites. How much these rites relate to the soul is particularly evident with death, where the soul leaves the body and, accompanied by the sound of the bell, must make the transition to a new form of existence.

Accompanying these transitions, the bell is endowed with magic powers, meaning that it wards off evil forces, which are automatically drawn to those awkward phases where the "old man" has run out of energy and the new one is not yet born. The transition into a new life situation calls for a new 'tuning', a new attitude turned towards the 'inside' or else directed from the 'inside', so that the new person must be different from the old one. Thus, for example, while the transition from single to married

91 P. Sartori, *Das Buch von deutschen Glocken,* p. 93.

status takes place within an external social framework, the tolling of the bell is a reminder that there is a parallel internal transition taking place at the same time.

In traditional village culture, any man leaving the ranks of the unmarried was forced by the others to pay a ransom, either in money or in kind. After that, there was no alternative but to join the new community of married couples. Today, these boundaries are blurred, and that also seems to be the case with the internal adjustment. The external terms of reference, laid down in custom and tradition, which denoted the important transition, have largely disappeared, and the inner ones, indicating the required new attitude to life, also often seem to have fallen by the wayside. The transition into the marital status is only successful to a limited degree for the young couple since this new status is still measured by the former mode of life. The result is frustration about the lost freedom as well as about the new responsibility. Young couples today certainly have the opportunity to live a life relatively free from conventional constraints, but at the same time they are saddled with the burden of having to make decisions which were previously made for them through established rules and regulations: "Shall we have children or not?", "How binding should our relationship be?", "Who is responsible for what?". These are momentous decisions, which often pose a major problem in a relationship. The trend towards the dissolving of traditional family structures and gender roles, bringing so-called patchwork families, with and without children, homosexual marriages, and so on, plus the demands of combining family and career placed on marriage partners with equal rights, all require entirely new life adjustments, unknown to the older generations.

The problem now is to find new *inner* terms of reference without the old external structures, but also without new external, collective opinions. An inner uncertainty about the way we shape our lives corresponds to the loss of external forms and rituals, just as an internal uprooting or inner homelessness can correspond to an external homelessness and restlessness. The inner sense of insecurity cannot, of course, be remedied simply by resurrecting the old customs and ways of life. For the external forms were only a vessel for internal, psychologically 'right and proper' values, just as the bells on the church tower were able to lend expression to an inner, guiding voice.

Today, liberation from the firmly established customs and structures of traditional community life has brought us more individual options. However, the new spirit of freedom can bring a restlessness and a rootlessness, which makes us like a shallow-rooted tree, unstable and vulnerable to wind and weather. This image corresponds to a state of consciousness detached from its instinctual base, and not only easily lost in exteriority and superficiality, but also tending to suggestibility and obsessiveness.

The bell is not always tied to its location. It is said to be able to change its position independently and often it can be heard over huge distances, which would not be possible in real life. The sound can be heard coming from the ground, from water, from mountains, the places that have always been considered the source of what is unknown and mysterious. In fairy tales, these are the places where witches, giants, dwarves, water nymphs and forest fairies dwell. They all represent the sphere of the unconscious, the home of the things we do not know that nevertheless affect us. Even today, a man may timidly start singing a song if he has to walk alone through a dark forest at night, like a child, or just as his archaic ancestors might have done. His response comes from a deep, unconscious area, where he himself has remained an archaic man. Since primeval times, the contents of the collective unconscious have preceded our consciousness, which is of a much more recent date. This is probably the reason why the bell is very often referred to as being of ancient origin, reaching back to pre-Christian times.We share with our distant ancestors the collective unconscious, from which the voice of the bell sounds. Folk traditions of past centuries must therefore not be simply dismissed as antiquated customs. Their value lies in their symbolic significance, even if to appreciate it we first have to distil the meaning from the original form and translate it into our psychological language.

In fairy tales, the bell sometimes crops up as having a protecting or warning function. In this role, it can be understood psychologically as sensitivity and attentiveness to inner things.[92] When the bells warn about storms, severe weather and war, then here, too, it is about the timely identification of destructive emotions from the unconscious, which can threaten not only the individual, but also a whole collective.

92 H. Beit and M.-L. von Franz, *Symbolik des Märchens*, p. 441.

The sound of the warning bell, especially for collective interests, appears quite frequently in dreams. A new publication by Theodor Abt is interesting in this context, presenting a complete set of modern dreams which highlights the unconscious background of the present collective situation in terms of a warning, but also as an outlook from the perspective of the unconscious.[93]

In several legends, the special value of the bell is conveyed by the fact that the ordinary metal of the so-called bell oil, the casting, is transformed into a more noble metal. Somehow silver, or even gold, is mixed into it. The chime of such a bell is said to be a special one. In actual fact, the bell sound would be destroyed somewhat by adding silver or gold. Gold was always known as a metal that does not corrode, even if it has been buried in the earth for hundreds or even thousands of years; hence its significance as something indestructible, of supreme value. Silver is the metal of the moon and is associated with the feminine, connecting principle. Therefore the addition of silver to the bell mixture symbolises contact with the night world of the moon. At certain times, or on certain feast days, the sound of the bells is conducive to divination, for example, and to all kinds of nocturnal magic. The bell itself often has the ability to prophesy. The bell sound thus connects the people in a mysterious way with the knowledge of the other world, or of the unconscious. Its effect, however, clearly depends on the *kairos*, the right moment in time, as we shall see.

In this context, the bell can be viewed as a symbol for what Jung refers to as the transcendent function of the psyche. It can be explained as follows: in the life process, there seems to be a kind of goal-oriented tendency to unite conscious and unconscious contents, with a view to establishing and maintaining emotional balance. Consciousness always tends to be one-sided in its focus and its temporary adjustment, and thus runs contrary to instinct. In view of this one-sidedness, and as we can see in the symbolic allusions of dreams, the unconscious appears to adopt a self-regulating, complementary or compensatory function. Here, too, the moment in which such a reaction from the unconscious appears is of great importance. This is why, in analysis, we should not attempt to open someone's eyes to a problem before that problem has been brought up by the unconscious itself, in a dream, for example. It is usually only then

93 See Th. Abt, *Dark Clouds over Europe. The latent Danger of renewed Tyranny.*

that anything new can be fully understood and implemented in life. The transcendent function enables us to hear the voice of the bell, to recognise the symbolic dimension of the statements from the unconscious and to connect them with our consciousness. Conscious and unconscious factors can then interact in a new and different way. An organic transition can be made from an attitude that has become one-sided to one which furthers development of the life process.[94]

Just how difficult it is to make a connection between the conscious and the unconscious spheres, and the dangers this may entail, can be seen in all the notions about the defensive and protective function of the bell. As its sound covers the whole of village life, with its day-to-day activities, its festivals, its laws and regulations, the bell protects everything that is part of the culture created by the people, in other words, the achievements of consciousness. Where the sound of the church bell is no longer heard, there is instead the so-called "golden ring", which in some mountain regions of Switzerland a peasant draws around the alp with the evening prayer call. This golden ring is intended to protect the alp, and its inhabitants and animals, against the overpowering forces of nature.[95]

The conscious sphere is always in danger of being swallowed up again by the surrounding unconscious. We have already noted that if we have had a new idea or a dream, we so easily lose it again and forget it, however much we would like to hang on to it. But it is too late! The moment has passed in which we could have worked on it. It has got away from us, as if it had never wanted to become conscious. This seems paradoxical, because everything that is really new comes creatively from the unconscious. Inner nature, like external nature, creates and destroys in a continuous cycle that only consciousness is able to break through. We do not know why consciousness developed in mankind or must continue to develop, but we know that the mysterious world of the unconscious, inhabited by spirits and demonic forces, has always represented a threat to man. As Jung says, people have always viewed the unconscious as *the* primeval danger, which explains all the primitive rituals for banishing

94 M.-L. von Franz, *C. G. Jung. His Myth in our Time*, p. 96f. And: C. G. Jung, "The Transcendent Function", in: *The Structure and the Dynamics of the Psyche* [CW 8], § 131-193.

95 Cf. E. Renner, *Goldener Ring über Uri.*

ghosts, exorcising spirits and warding off evil omens, for purification and for magical conjuring favourable events. They serve to strengthen consciousness.[96] The bell has the same function, where the unconscious sphere represents a threat to consciousness.

There are occasions when we have to trust an inner voice, which warns us about the unconscious taking over, whether it is within ourselves, or whether in relation to dealing with someone in danger of being overwhelmed by his affects. Sometimes all we can do is to try and turn attention away from the unconscious and to defuse the situation. With children, this works wonderfully well. Assuming that we can see the storm brewing, we can often, with a little imagination, quite easily distract a little child who threatens to work himself up into a rage and make a big scene. Then the whole thing collapses and the overpowering emotion is banished. Whether or not this ruse succeeds, depends to a large extent on how well we sense what is going on below the surface, in our 'bell sensorium', as it were, only a small part of which is subordinate to our conscious will. If, in such a moment, we instinctively succeed in doing the right thing, it often means disturbance in the relationship can be avoided.

Although the bell is actually man-made, in popular belief it acts as an independent, rational personality with a mind of its own. It is master of its voice and even of its own movement, it punishes abuse, is fair, grateful, pious, socially-minded and so on. It has a name, very often that of a saint. Through the bell, the saint himself speaks, as mediator of the divine will. And so the bell 'voice' becomes the *vox Dei*, the voice of God. The words *Vox Dei* or *Vox Domini* were, in fact, inscribed on some old church bells before they were melted down for weapons production in war.[97]

96 See C.G. Jung, *The Archetypes and the Collective Unconscious* [CW 9/I], § 47.

97 The inscription on the bell of the cathedral of St. Nikolai von Greifswald (DE) from the year 1568 reads as follows: «VOX EGO VOX VITE VOCO ORARE VENITE. (I am the voice, the voice of life. I call to you, come and pray.)»
On the Barbara-Bell in the St. Barbara Church in Mülheim-Dümpten it says: «VOX MEA! VOX DEI! AUDITE! VENITE! (My voice! The voice of God! Listen! Come!)». It was first cast in 1894, newly cast in 1956.

Fig. 28: Bell Founder. Christoph Weigel. Copper Engraving, 1711.

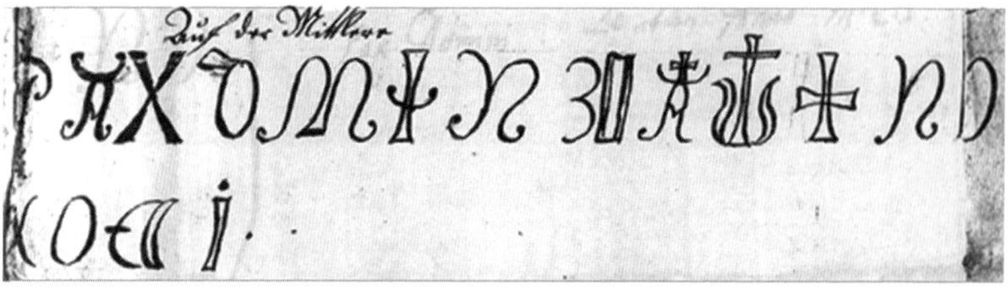

Fig. 29: Inscription bell of the church St. Johannes, Obhausen (DE): «PAX DOMINI – VOX DEI».[98]

For the believer, it was clear what was meant by the *vox Dei*. For most people, however, this is no longer the case. Since it is from the human psyche that the concept of the voice of God has emerged, it can also be approached from the viewpoint of psychology. Where and how does man experience something like the voice of God? Jung explains that the *vox Dei* can simply be another expression for human conscience. By conscience we usually mean something that torments us if we have done something we assume we should not have done, according to the general acceptance of what is right and wrong. However, conscience, as the voice of God, is a much broader concept. This conscience can weigh heavily on us even if nobody is threatening to punish us, and we do not necessarily know why it makes its presence felt in a particular situation. According to C.G. Jung, this kind of conscience is an archetypal phenomenon of numinous character, which possesses incomparably higher authority than traditional morality or the dictates of religion, society and culture. The *vox Dei*, which can express itself in the voice of conscience, is an autonomous and dynamic psychic factor that commands the individual to obey, even at the risk of going astray, because, like a biological phenomenon, it is morally indifferent.[99] This 'autonomous' conscience, which Jung distinguishes from the Christian moral conscience, is expressed by the symbol of the bell, which, according to ancient folk beliefs, has its own notions of

98 Enlarged resolution sign of the medieval «PAX DOMINI...VOX DEI» inscription (14th century) of the bell in Obhausen (Querfurt, DE). At the end of the inscription: «VOX» with an upside down U instead of a V. Such 'errors' are typical of medieval bells. I owe this information Dr. Konrad Noll. The Bell was melted down for weapons production.

99 C.G.. Jung, "A Psychological View of Conscience". In: *Civilisation in Transition* [CW 10], § 842ff.

right and wrong. It leads to a kind of ethical assessment of action, which goes beyond the general moral consensus of what is good and what is evil. The voice of the bell, which we have referred to as conveying a higher knowledge, is, like the 'autonomous' conscience, not something that comes from the ego, but refers to «an unconscious personality [... which], to all appearances, behaves like a conscious subject.»[100]

It is common knowledge that oaths were sworn on bells in the administration of justice, the view being that such oaths were indisputable. Any perjurer could expect very severe punishment. Oaths sworn on a bell were even more common than those sworn on the Gospel. The bell, as the *vox Dei*, which can also wreak terrible vengeance for any disregard of the Gospel, represents an irrefutable higher authority. The "unconscious personality" expresses itself here as inner law, which, if ignored, has serious consequences. The guidelines for this law are not issued by some external power; they manifest through an irrational feeling that something is right or wrong, regardless of whether it is good or evil in the strictly moral sense. Occasionally we can see that a person should acknowledge the direction of this unconscious law because it presents itself clearly in his dreams. For some reason, perhaps because of repressed fear, he misunderstands it or stubbornly disregards it. He may have a "guilty conscience", but he excuses himself, for example, because he did not come up to the expectations of society or the family, or because, in his opinion, external circumstances are to blame. The long-term consequences for him may be serious psychological crises or physical illness.

So the voice of the bell has to do with guidance from the unconscious. Legends tell how the sound of bells showed the way home to people who had lost their way and thus saved them from destruction. In some places, there were even so-called 'Irrglocken', bells which used to ring out at certain times to help people lost in snow, fog, marshland and forest to find their way back home.[101] It was also believed that mysterious bells could lead people astray, just as the sound of the bell not only offered protection against bad weather, but could also attract it.

100 Ibid., § 829.

101 P. Sartori, *Das Buch von Deutschen Glocken.* p. 53.

As we have seen, consciousness can be repeatedly threatened by the unconscious. Getting lost in a swamp or in a forest is a suitable image for what can happen when ego-consciousness can no longer see its way, is at its wits' end, or is bogged down in crisis or depression. But sometimes the colourful contents of the unconscious can also be so overwhelming or fascinating that a person cannot find his way back into everyday life. This danger lurks behind any kind of addiction, but also today behind the fascination with computer games and other virtual fantasy products, which often seem to come from an irrational dream world and to give a neurotically distorted view of reality. Legends tell of an eerie bell sound in nature which misleads people and separates them from reality. In contrast, just as the chime from the church bell-tower was the best and easiest way to show a lost person the way back to his home village, it was the call of the conscious everyday world, and the guidance of Christian consciousness in particular, which could counter the risk of the unconscious getting out of hand.

The church tower can be understood as the Christian dogma, which, as Jung pointed out, together with ritual, has «since time immemorial, been a safe way of dealing with the unpredictable forces of the unconscious».[102] «They [the dogmas] replace the immediate religious experience of the people by a choice of suitable symbols, so that they do not have to decide whether the experience came from God or from the devil, and whether it is to be accepted or rejected.»[103] Since immediate experience of the unconscious can easily be too much for an individual, making him vulnerable to overwhelming fear, conflict, depression, or even madness, it is important and useful, according to Jung, for a practising believer to remain within the Church, as long as it works for him.[104]

For people today, the protective walls of the Church are often crumbling and its bells have been silenced. Many can no longer simply believe, and the symbolic content of religious statements is incomprehensible to them. What is missing for them is a convincing

102 C. G. Jung, "Psychology and Religion". In: *Psychology and Religion: West and East* [CW 11], § 82.

103 Ibid., § 75.

104 Ibid., § 79.

religious experience, an experience that nobody else can prove or disprove to them. Such an experience ultimately comes from one's own soul background. It is from there, or, in symbolic language, from the forest, the water, the swamp, that the bell as the *vox Dei* can be heard. It represents the experience of a superior, inner knowledge, which points the way forward and is meaningful. However the place where the bell is located is dangerous. Turning to this voice is frightening when it comes from our unconscious inner nature, rather than from the church tower or from some other religious structure. It can call forth things that we are afraid of because they do not match our familiar Christian understanding of good and evil.

The *vox Dei* is above human law and the general moral code which regulate our conduct. Like the bell, it abides by its own laws and its own notion of right and wrong. The voice of this 'absolute' conscience can therefore appear evil, sinister and seductive. It often sees the guidance of our 'clear conscience' in a very different light. Under certain circumstances, it may call for an ethical decision, one which does not question the values of good and evil, but, coming as it does from the unconscious instinctual base of the psyche, it is not identical with our traditional moral standards. Let us think, for example, of a captain in the last days of the Second World War who, despite the orders of the 'Führer' and knowing that he might be shot, orders his soldiers to retreat from a hopeless battle. He is in the agonising moral dilemma of choosing between obedience to his superiors and his country, and a human accountability to his subordinates. The difficult choice in this conflict is an ethical decision that can only come from the inner personality. According to Jung, an ethical decision becomes a «subjective and creative act», but one which calls for «a spontaneous and decisive impulse on the part of the unconscious.»[105]

This impetus from the unconscious may simply manifest in a special feeling, which would add the dimension of the soul to the views dictated by conscious opinions. In a dispute, for example, a person can be in the right and yet still offend the other party, and a personal feeling – a kind of inner voice – could tell him so, if it were not drowned out by the cries of his own dogmatic side. Or there are occasions when we really do not feel or sense what we should do, and cannot make up our minds.

105 C. G. Jung, *Memories, Dreams, Reflections,* p. 330f.

The voice of reason or external circumstances requires a certain decision, while our feelings are contradictory and uncertain. Then we are faced with a real dilemma. In such a situation, it is sometimes useful to bear with the conflict, to let time pass, to do nothing for the moment. This gives the unconscious a chance to come up with a solution. When it comes, this solution is usually quite unexpected, yet entirely in accordance with reality, from an unconventional but life-enhancing point of view.

Whenever people identify too strongly with what is socially correct, they lose their connection with this dynamic reality. General rules and collective ideas then become merely 'opinions', empty words, which can repress natural instinct and lead to neurotic malfunctioning. On the collective level, this problem is evident today in the flood of state by-laws and regulations affecting almost every level of daily life. It means that self-regulation in the individual, and also in the community, is becoming more and more a thing of the past. The voice of the bell, and so the transcendent function, the self-regulating function of the unconscious, is over-ridden. What we have is purely and simply a collective neurosis.

Let us recall how we are influenced by the external moral code. Our culture and religion have set up rules of conduct which are passed on to each child. The point of this is to organize our collective life. Children learn to subordinate themselves to these rules and, in so doing, they grow up with established notions of what is right and wrong in life. They continue to acquire these ideas until adulthood, and so gain the impression that the ideas are their own, even when they are not based on their own experience. Later in life, they have a bad conscience whenever they overstep the bounds of the established rules, even though their inner voice, their own 'gut feeling' might say something completely different. Then a person may suddenly no longer be so sure about what should be done. The previously solid moral pillars of conscience seem to be shaky. What often happens next is that uncertainty turns into a hardening of consciousness, with a rigid defending of the old ideas. However, a degree of honesty might bring the latent, seemingly irreconcilable conflict to light, the conflict between what 'should be' in accordance with external requirements and the demands of one's own inner voice.

A modern woman, for example, can often be found in such a difficult situation when she needs to assert herself in the male working world. The magic word 'equality', which is supposed to liberate her and offer her equal opportunities, may also put her under enormous pressure. What is often actually freed is the animus, the masculine side of woman. The animus does help the woman to survive in the male world, it is true, but what may get lost in the process is her own feminine 'gut feeling'. Genuine empowerment of women would ultimately mean a new awareness of inner things. It would mean restoring connection to the voice of the bell. But truly independent womanhood is unlikely be achieved without that same conflict between what she should do and what she would like to do in accordance with general expectations and the unknown factor from the depths of her own soul, which is sure to throw a spanner in the works. While a man in the rational masculine professional world is usually able to repress his gut feelings for longer than a woman, without suffering any ill effects, for her, suppressing the inner voice can soon give rise to an overt emotional or physical problem. The increasing number of 'burnouts', which have become a kind of modern 'folk disease', do, however, show that more and more men are apparently suffering from this problem too.

Wherever life involves us in such a conflict, the old feeling of security has gone by the board. Remaining with the image of the legend, there is only the perilous route into nature, from where, far away, the voice of the bell still sounds. Through this connection to the unconscious, our way of adapting to outer life, which has lost its absolute validity, can be brought closer to the compelling new inner reality. This way is dangerous because the encounter with the *vox Dei,* which, as an autonomous internal factor, need not match our conscious perceptions, can plunge us into a painful rethinking process or into a new venture in life. Experience of the *vox Dei* can give a feeling of "I must do it", even if it does not make sense. Then the question is simply: is this "I must do it" right, or actually wrong? Am I running after a misleading 'errant bell'? So the crucial question becomes: how do we cope with the unconscious and how can a genuinely ethical decision be made? I would like to dig deeper into this question.

Let us look again at the dream by which the inner voice can express itself. If it is correctly understood by consciousness, it conveys unexpected knowledge that is life-enriching. However, if it is misunderstood, real harm can be done and it can wreak havoc. It may also be that the inner voice is driving us towards something that we must reject, and with good reason, something that we experience as an overpowering inner compulsion which affects our judgement. The voice from the unconscious then becomes the one deceiving us, the trickster, Satan or an evil spirit, which is how early man explained the destructive influence of the unconscious.

Jung says that the primeval form of conscience is intrinsically a morally ambivalent, archetypal reaction of the collective unconscious. In other words, it has no moral attributes. It is pure nature: neither good nor evil. Only when the impulses of conscience penetrate into consciousness do they acquire a moral quality. Only then can consciousness decide whether this autonomous conscience is right or wrong in terms of conventional morality, whether, for example, its motives are selfish or calculating or not. The right decision may not be immediately obvious. You can have a guilty conscience where it is not justified, or do bad things with a clear conscience. Then the bell's voice misleads you. The only thing that is clear is the psychological statement that this primeval conscience has greater authority than conventional morality. It is stronger than any argument based on reason. As Jung says, it is an autonomous psychological factor, an archetypal force which can seriously challenge conventional morality. It can either be described in positive terms as a *daemon*, *genius*, guardian angel, heart, better self, inner voice, inner or higher man, and so forth, or then as devil, seducer, evil spirit, etc.[106] Like all archetypes, it exerts a very strong influence on human behaviour. M.-L. von Franz says: «I have yet to see the unconscious make really profound immoral demands; however, it is part of nature and cares little for petty social rules.»[107] Ultimately, it is only an independent, discerning consciousness that can identify this nature and treat it with the seriousness that it merits. Only such consciousness can reach a constructive, ethical decision with regard to unconscious dynamics. That also means consciously accepting uncertainties, questioning one's own point of view, weighing up different possibilities. Decisions arrived at in an individual way may not always be understood by others, but because they are supported by the unconscious they are usually effective.

Back to the bell. As we have seen, it is, so to speak, a vessel or

106 C.G. Jung, "A Psychological View of Conscience". In: *Civilisation in Transition* [CW 10], § 843-845.

107 M.-L. von Franz, "Jung's Discovery of the Self". In: *Archetypal Dimensions of the Psyche*, p. 366.

'switchboard' for the *vox Dei*, enabling it to be heard in the conscious world. That is why it is anchored in the everyday human world, attached to its location. Only in connection to the world of consciousness can it fulfil its function; only through consciousness can an unconscious impulse be recognised at all. If we are not very conscious, we usually notice too late or not at all that our behaviour is once again beyond our control and the unconscious has taken over. The mediating function of the bell was not working; it would have passed on the overpowering impulse in a carefully measured out, maybe even comprehensible form. But we did not recognise it in time. Given that the bell belongs to the human world, the *vox Dei* is dependent on human beings via the bell. This reminds us of gods who must be fed and dressed, regardless of their divine abilities, as they would otherwise starve and have to go naked. Through this relatedness to the all-powerful gods, their dangerous despotism is pacified. In the Ancient Orient, the mother goddess *Aruru* created man so that with corn meal and flour he could make bread for the gods, who till then had only been able to drink water. This myth says that without the care and attention of the people, the gods have no access to human life. It is even the Mother Goddess herself who instigated the creation of man for this purpose. What this means psychologically is that the unconscious itself is interested in a relationship with consciousness so that the archetypes can find expression – in both their creative and destructive dynamics – in a humanly intelligible manner. Relationship to these archetypal powers is what makes it possible in the first place for there to be a growth and development of consciousness, aimed at countering its unpredictable force.

The bell, seen as a feeling or 'sensorium', helps to bring about that relatedness. It can mediate between consciousness and anything that overpoweringly affects or influences us from the unconscious in both a positive and a negative way. But here, too, it is ultimately critical awareness which must listen to the voice of the bell and take it seriously, in order to be able to sense whether it will bring in the will of benevolent or less benevolent gods, whether it announces treasures or storms, thunderstorms, landslides and floods. In other words: where the relationship to the unconscious is alive, its destructive element can also become evident. Then one must sometimes allow a critical moment to pass, without 'touching' the unconscious. Viewed psychologically, forces of nature embody archetypal energies from the unconscious – overpowering forces, for which we are no match 'once they are released'.[108]

There are occasions therefore, according to popular belief, when the bells have to be allowed to fall silent. This is the case if there is a possibility that their sound might bring on a storm, with thunder and lightning, and the risk of fire and flood. Sometimes there needs to be a conscious decision not to give free rein to whatever is trying to break out from within, not to let the storm erupt, as it might be too destructive. There are also moments when we would actually like to have all the alarm bells ringing, when we want to shout out our feelings of anger and hatred, or expose the fears and dark thoughts that have gathered inside us like thunder-clouds. It can be difficult to hold back such an apparently liberating outburst, but there is no telling how much harm it could do. The unconscious can also throw us into a state of panic, and panic is always blind and self-destructive. It is also contagious and therefore dangerous on the collective level. All feelings and emotions that erupt spontaneously from the unconscious, have, as we have seen in the example of fire, this dangerously contagious and unpredictable aspect. Sometimes the bell has to be silenced, closing the door to the unconscious. In analysis, it is mainly borderline cases who can present the analyst with the difficult decision whether or not the door to the unconscious must be closed, because a weak ego-consciousness, like a fragile house, might be unable to withstand the impending storm.

The relationship of man to the bells was formerly of great importance. This we know from sagas in which they were misused; the recasting of bells into cannons is especially remembered as a shameful act.[109] Other legends tell how the bells were hidden and thus saved at the last moment before they were evacuated. Sartori paints a moving picture of the so-called 'dying of the bells' in Germany in 1917, which he himself still recalled. All the church bells were requisitioned for melting down for cannons. He describes harrowing scenes in the villages as locals had to bid farewell to their bells, crowning them with wreaths for the last service, touching them all for the last time, stroking them, scraping off

108 The Bell inscription on the Schaffhausen Minster Bell, chosen by Friedrich Schiller as his motto for his *Song of the Bell*, was: «VIVOS VOCO MORTUOS PLANGO FULGURA FRANGO (I call the living, I pity the dead, I break up the bolts of lightning)».

109 P. Sartori, *Das Buch von deutschen Glocken,* p. 131.

Fig. 30: Inscription on the bell of the Schaffhausen minster, the "Schillerglocke".

their metal and picking it up, and standing in the streets looking on as they were carried away. In places where the bells had to be hurled down from the tower, it was like a murder that «made all the onlookers shudder in horror. One parish was so outraged and infuriated at the requisitioning of its bells that it was only after the situation had been explained to them in the sermon and in conversation that they finally calmed down.»[110]

In this last example, it was the 'enlightenment', i.e. a one-sided purpose-oriented consciousness, which made the separation from the bell possible. If we take into account all that the bells meant to people emotionally, this was a sudden and brutal severing from the realm of the unconscious. Apparently there were also pastors, standard-bearers of the Christian Church, playing an active role in this 'enlightenment'. It was not only the pastors, but also the teachers, the whole intellectual elite, who were behind the irrational war euphoria, with which the young volunteers

110 Ibid., p. 134.

jubilantly marched off to the Front and to death.[111] They seemed to be totally unaware of the terrible consequences of war and saw no reason to distrust the slogans of those in power, who were spurring them on. The voice of the bell was silenced. The great suffering of the First World War was followed about twenty years later by that of the Second, in which, once again, an entire nation had lost its connection to the unconscious and, under the powerful influence of the archetype that consequently emerged, allowed itself to be dragged down into destruction. In the First World War, some 40'000 church bells were melted down and in the Second World War the figure was around 60'000, these bells often the very ones purchased by parishes at great sacrifice after the first war.

Our connection to the inner voice is always in danger of getting lost. This is reflected in all the legends about bells sunken in the earth, or lost in meadow, water, mountain or forest, and often ringing mysteriously.[112] This type of legend is closely related to the legends about treasure troves and to those about the White Lady, an unredeemed feminine figure that appears in many legends and fairytales. Instead of treasure, fishermen may find a bell in their nets, for example, as they drag them out of the water. Bells sunken in water and in the earth illustrate the need to be saved. But salvation often fails, and people involved in the recovery of the bells come up against great difficulties. Bells that have been raised may return to the water, because apparently the time is not yet right for them: «Not yet, Margret, man wedder so deep!» is what two bells shout to each other, having been lifted from a lake by a fisherman on Saint John's Day. Whereupon they had plunged back into the lake. Or a bell shouts: «Hanne Susanne kommt nümmermeer zu Lanne.»[113]

What the testimony of sunken treasures, bells and White Ladies have in common is that a precious, collective value once present has, over time, sunk into the earth, forest, mountain or lake, i.e. into the unconscious, and is there awaiting redemption. Fortunately, the legends also tell us what

111 C. Zuckmayer, *Als wär's ein Stück von mir.* See the impressive biography of the author. In the First World War he moved to the Front as an enthusiastic 17-year-old.

112 *Handwörterbuch des deutschen Aberglaubens*, vol. III, 873f.

113 P. Sartori, *Das Buch von deutschen Glocken,* p. 175 and p. 178. «Again (wedder) into the depths (deep).» It is clear that the bells vanished back into the depths. And: «Hanne Susanne does not return to land.»

Fig. 31: Church bells delivered to be melted down at the station of Fürstenfeldbruck (DE), 20. July 1917.

it takes to redeem this precious value. And here, amazingly enough, we come across the pig once more. Legends, but also sayings or inscriptions on bells themselves, tell how each one had been found and excavated by a pig. The location is often assumed to be the site of a now sunken city.[114]

Many church bells, especially in the Alpine countries, are also called the sow and are given names. The Witterschwander weather Bell in the Schächen Valley is called 'Santä Toni-Sywli' (i.e. Antonius piglet). In J. Müller's *Tales from Uri*, several variations can be found of the legend which tells of the landslide or avalanche that the witches intend to bring down on the valley. There the bell begins to ring in the village and the witches have to abandon their project: «Ds Sywli gysset, mer chennet nytt mache», or «ds Santä Toni-Sywli gysset».[115] So here together we have St. Antonius, the pig and the bell!

114 Ibid., p. 178.

115 The piglet calls, we cannot do anything! Or: The St. Antonius piglet calls! J. Müller, *Sagen aus Uri,* No. 192, 195, 201, 203. See also G. Isler, *Die Sennenpuppe.*

Fig. 32: Storage of church bells in the Hamburg docks, 1947.

The pig, as we have seen, is closely connected to the earth. It sniffs around in the dirt and digs up precious things like truffles, or even whole treasure troves. It has a fine nose for anything valuable that lies buried in the ground, such as the stone of the alchemists, which they said was to be found (*invenitur in stercore*) in manure. There, in the manure, the most despised place, is where the most valuable thing of all was believed to be hidden. In psychological terms, we can equate manure with the unconscious shadow side of human nature, or even with the unconscious itself, which has been held in low esteem, ignored and – especially when modern psychology was in its infancy – was regarded as the dumping ground for everything dirty and repressed. And yet, as with the manure, it is precisely there where the most precious thing can be found. In the Christian tradition, the pig, as we have seen, has lost many of the positive associations that it had in pre-Christian times. To have a place that is "like a pigsty" is something that no respectable human being would like to be accused of, something verging on the immoral. There is no place for the pig within the framework of our moral code. And yet, according to the message from the unconscious in legend and popular belief, it is precisely this creature that can trace the inner voice – or higher conscience – and allow it to be heard again. Legends and popular beliefs convey thoughts and images unacknowledged in Christian consciousness, but in accord with man's instinctive nature, as we can see from dreams, fantasies and visions.

Sometimes articulating and consciously accepting a totally 'impossible' or distressing situation, or chaotic ideas and thoughts, or a strange or unpleasant dream, can bring a feeling of relief and a release of tension. The connection to the inner voice is established and, unexpectedly, an inner harmony is restored, a sense of vitality returns and energy starts to flow again. This experience of peace and wellbeing soon passes, however, for it is virtually impossible for ego-consciousness to be constantly open to what the inner voice has to say. Loss of the inner voice manifests, for example, in the feeling of not being at one with oneself, in feeling irritable for no obvious reason, or dissatisfied with oneself, or not 'in tune' with oneself. Finding the inner voice often means having to deal with matters that are unfamiliar or unpleasant, that seek space in our psychological house, even if they threaten to make it look 'like a pigsty'. The lost inner voice thus has a lot to do with the unconscious instincts, dynamic factors on which, as Jung says, the ethical decisions of our consciousness ultimately depend.[116]

According to legend, it is sometimes farmers or shepherds who find the bell again. In their dealings with nature and animals, farmers and shepherds rely on their instinctive connectedness, on their 'nose' for the things of nature. In other words, it is apparently a natural instinct-related attitude that is in harmony with the demands of nature, in tune with the inner voice. Sometimes the bell can be found by a blind man, someone for whom the light no longer shines, but who "sees in the dark", so to speak. The blind man represents feeling and intuition, which are closer to the twilight of the unconscious than the bright lights of reason and understanding. So in relating to inner nature those softer, more subtle functions of consciousness are often more helpful than the clarity of intellect. The same can be true in analysis, where, for example, often little or nothing is achieved with words. Analysands may nod in agreement

116 C.G. Jung, *Memories, Dreams Reflections,* p. 330.

and give the impression of understanding everything, but somehow you can sense that nothing has really sunk in and their feeling has not been touched. A person may have studied psychology for years and yet not have picked up very much about the essence of the psyche, because, despite all his knowledge, he is lacking in emotional experience. That is a big drawback in our one-sided, intellectual, university training of psychologists, who should actually be responsible for understanding the voice of the unconscious.

Let us recall that folk tradition speaks of the origin of the bells in ancient times. The fact that there often used to be a town in the place where the sunken bell is found also suggests that in ancient times the bell was part of a culture now submerged. There must have been something there of collective spiritual and cultural value, working in tandem with the unconscious. The motif of a sunken city, a forgotten castle, and so on, crops up so frequently in legends and fairy tales that we can assume there must be a special meaning behind it. In several of his works, Jung states that in the early days of Christianity its symbols, for the people in those times, still completely fulfilled the function of a connection to the unconscious. This means that the unconscious of those people was expressed in the symbolic language of Christianity in a perfectly adequate way. But with the passage of time and with the increasing institutionalisation of the Church, the living language of symbols became bogged down in dogmas, where, although it still expressed eternal truths, it was less and less accessible to the understanding of minds that were steadily developing. For the consciousness of modern man, the dogmas have usually completely lost their significance; their language is no longer understood. A city has sunk into the unconscious.

Over the centuries, the new symbols that emerged in visions and beliefs unrelated to the Church were often condemned by the Church as heresy and were suppressed. Consequently in the latter part of the Christian era it has become more difficult for the unconscious to be able to exert its compensatory influence, which sought to balance the one-sidedness of the ecclesiastical perspective. The active formation of symbols, the active exchange between unconscious contents and conscious outer life, was increasingly lost. The consequence was that the inner voice, the bell voice, disappeared from the Church. It sank into the lake, the forests, the earth, and although it may sometimes still be heard from a distance, it is very hard to find it again. According to a Swiss legend from the Valais, dating back to the 15th century, the bell was even lost to the Pope in Rome! One version of the shortened legend goes like this:

Theodul, Bishop St. Jodern of Sion, who had been of service to the Pope and in Rome, had requested a large bell in return, "which is useful for the weather." But this bell was sunk deep into the ground, and no one knew where it was. So the Bishop asked it to ring, which it did, and so it could be dug up. Whereupon the Bishop Jodern ordered the Devil to carry the bell all the way from Rome to Sion in the canton of Valais, where ever since, it has worked wonders in dealing with severe weather.[117]

Sometimes, even the Devil has to help to bring the lost bell's voice home! This legend was probably recounted with a pinch of salt, because here, too, as so often in legends, the Devil is given quite an important role, a role that the Church had not necessarily planned for him. The special authority of Bishop Joder could apparently deal with the Devil and gave new life to the bell, helping the mountain people to cope better with the unpredictable forces of nature.

Since the Enlightenment, the voice of the bell has increasingly been deprived of its *raison d'*être as a psychic reality. There are still bells to be found in church steeples and the Christian doctrine still speaks of the voice of God, but for fewer and fewer people is this of any importance. The firmness of faith, that characterised the spiritual attitude of past centuries, is known to many now only from hearsay. Parents and teachers, if they are honest with themselves, are usually embarrassed if they are called upon to answer children's questions about why we believe in God, who Jesus was, or what religion is. Jung's formulation strikes me as helpful here, because it is not limited to predetermined notions, but transfers the question to the inner level, which is the only place where it really makes sense.

He says: «Religion appears to me to be a peculiar attitude of mind which could be formulated in accordance with the original use of the word '*religio*', which means a careful consideration and observation of

117 J. Guntern, *Walliser Sagen,* p. 25.

Fig. 33: St. Theodul with the bell. Painting owned by the Domkapitel of Sitten (CH).

certain dynamic factors that are conceived as 'powers': spirits, daemons, gods, laws, ideas, ideals, or whatever name man has given to such factors in his world as he has found powerful, dangerous, or helpful enough to be taken into careful consideration, or grand, beautiful, and meaningful enough to be devoutly worshipped and loved.» These factors convey the experience of the *numinosum* to human consciousness and, in so doing, transform it.[118] It is apparently not only in our time that the experience of the numinous has been lost, for old legends say it can be recovered via the medium of animals or people in touch with their instincts, a category into which Bishop Joder would also almost certainly fall. So, according to the statements from the unconscious itself, it is the path of Nature, or the unconscious psyche, which can once again lead back to the *religio*, to the experience and careful consideration of the divine.

It is probably no coincidence that today so many young people are turning to farming, nature conservation and the country life. Nor perhaps is it surprising that we are seeing new ways of conducting rituals, which indicate that meaningless, rigid formalities are crumbling. For example, while it may be unconventional, it is no longer rare these days for wedding and funeral ceremonies to be held outdoors in the countryside. Such an innovation probably addresses a real need to approach numinous experience in a more individual, and natural way.

Fig. 34: Wedding ritual under a lime tree.

118 C. G. Jung, "Psychology and Religion". In: *Psychology of Religion, West and East* [CW 11], § 8f.

For modern man, *religio* or the consideration of factors that convey the experience of the divine, has shifted into the psychic space, the inner nature. It is therefore usually not enough to retire to the country or to an area of the world that is still archaic, imagining that it is an exemplary life simply because it is not destructive. For even there, nobody is immune from projecting his unconscious, destructive tendencies, meaning, first of all, everything in his own shadow that is repressed, unacceptable, inferior. On the contrary, the more one is inclined to believe that one lives a better and more correct life, the easier it is to fall into the trap of believing that others have got it all wrong. One then becomes fanatical in defence of one's principles. Contradictions are ripped open and, instead of the harmony and perfection he would like to see, the do-gooder may in fact merely be triggering conflict and aggression. And the Devil is once again laughing up his sleeve.

As we have seen, however, it can also be dangerous simply to give free rein to the inner nature. The idea of breaking free of old constraints and rigid forms, and allowing the natural man to live is, of course, positive. But underestimating the dark unconscious world to which one can also be delivered, removes the ground from under one's feet. New lifestyles do not just mean liberation, but often bring uncertainty, disorientation and depression as well. In popular sentiment, the figure of Bishop Joder embodies robust and sturdy dealings in relation to the devil, or to the evil in human nature. «In legends, there was a very differentiated knowledge of otherworldly powers, knowledge about how one had to behave, so that these powers brought one happiness and blessing and did not destroy one.»[119] In connection with bell legends, this means a constant questioning whether we understand the bell's voice correctly, so that it does not become a misleading errant bell.

When I was already working on this book, I had a dream about a sunken bell of incalculable value, which was kept in a central location, namely in the Gotthard mountain range, inside a mountain. It was looked after by a peasant who lived in a room crammed with books, like a library. All I could see were the books, the bell itself not being visible. As, at that moment, I was anyway concerned with bells and books, I was trying

119 G. Isler, *Lumen Naturae,* p. 278.

to track down the dream image. Alpine peasants used to lead a lonely life, which entailed great deprivation and they were constantly aware of the dangers in nature to which they and their cattle were exposed. Had they not had an instinctive sense for what "was in the air" – an imminent storm, an unexpected snow, a rockfall – and for how to deal with these natural dramas, they not could not have coped with the demands and responsibilities of life on the alp. In the dream, the farmer seems therefore to represent a spiritual authority who guards the knowledge of our culture preserved in the unconscious. The values embedded in this knowledge can be found there again and, through these values, the lost bell can be found again. Thus the place where the sunken, misunderstood, intellectual knowledge of our ancestors lies, is also, according to the dream, the lost access to the *vox Dei.*

For me, the lost knowledge of our culture included the entire span of folk wisdom with which I was currently occupied. However, I may not yet have recognised the book knowledge in its whole symbolic meaning, which is why the dream attached such importance to it. For me, as for many people today, the symbolic language had become difficult to understand. But this means that all the natural knowledge it contains about the functioning of the human psyche sinks back into the unconscious. This knowledge is disappearing from everyday life and is actually only to be found on the bookshelves of dusty libraries.[120]

I therefore understood that the knowledge expressed in symbolic form in ancient folk wisdom had to be translated into a new language. It is undeniably true that, in the modern era, we have made enormous strides in science and research. We have acquired technical knowledge which has given us unprecedented power over nature, but, in relation to the psyche, the inner nature, we still function as our ancestors did. Unfortunately, our current overvaluation of the practical and rational aspects of consciousness

120 Thanks to the untiring enthusiasm of collectors and generations of researchers, starting during the Romantic Period with the Brothers Grimm via W. Mannhardt and W. H. Riehl, to name but a few from the early days of folklore, we now have a huge amount of material on the subject. But even contemporary folklorists know less and less about what to do with it, which is why today, in the field of folklore, there is great uncertainty about their objectives. There is a compilation of this research material by Ingeborg Weber-Kellermann, *Deutsche Volkskunde* (German folklore). See also the modern work of Nikola Patzel *Symbole im Landbau* (Symbols in Farming*)* on W. Mannhardt's ethnographic survey of agriculture in Switzerland, which includes the psychological method of interpretation by C. G. Jung.

means we have tended to neglect our capacity to appreciate and to deal with the invisible and irrational things in life.

Let us return to Antonius. We know from medieval pictures and statues that one of his attributes is the book. Interpreting his book as a volume of traditional knowledge about matters of the soul may sound somewhat far-fetched, but in the medieval iconography of Antonius it is not without a certain justification. In general, Antonius' book is regarded the first compilation of rules for monks to originate in Egypt, though it is attributed largely to his pupils and admirers. According to the legends, Antonius, who also had the surname of *Abbas* (father of the monks), is said to have based his book of rules on life in the first monastery, which he founded. In fact, the founder of the original monastery and the first, strictly regulated monastic community was St. Pachomius, the second famous Egyptian father of monks born forty years after Antonius. In contrast to Pachomius, Antonius personified the individual and was a role model for the monastic life in seclusion, rather than in community.

Like the other desert fathers of the time, Antonius was serious about Christianity being a practical way of life. For these hermits, there was something fragile about Christian thinking that lived only in people's minds and could not be implemented in real life. So they created a counterweight to the one-sided religious and philosophical precepts of the churchmen of the day. Christianity was largely a theoretical matter in the Constantinian era (4th century) and a person's state of blessedness depended on acknowledgement of a dogmatic formula. The reclusive existence of the anchorites was a compensation for this. It was based not on philosophical exercises, but solely on individual experience, something which had been grossly neglected in the popular Christianity of the time. «The mediocre lazy slacker keeps it [the individual experience] at arm's length. It is so much easier to teach correctly than to live correctly.» wrote Walter Nigg in his biography of Antonius, not mincing his words.[121] This is as true today as it was then. It can be said that desert monks like Antonius, running counter to the intellectual 'mainstream', strove to listen to the inner voice, the *vox Dei*, and thus breathed new life into contemporary Christianity.

121 W. Nigg, *Vom Geheimnis der Mönche,* p. 62.

Here we must make a detour back to the dream at our starting point. We recall that the church bells were not making a harmonious sound and people walked out of the church. It seems that the bell voice, the inner voice and thus the voice of the self, can no longer be heard within the collective framework of the Church. The clashing of the bells corresponds to division and confusion within the Church, caused by the various contradictory religious ideas and opinions, and by the general uncertainty about the meaning and relevance of religious tradition that is characteristic of our age. This current crisis mirrors the religious situation at the time of Antonius, when there was much dogmatic discussion and speculation about the correct interpretation of Christianity.

According to the dream about the peasant in the Gotthard mountain range, the real bell is hidden inside the mountain and that is where it must be rediscovered. The symbolism of mountain, farmer and bell points to the search for the individual within, just as Antonius was looking for the path to his inner life as a hermit. The initial dream made no mention of a direct connection between Antonius and the bell. And yet the two parts of the dream are linked together. After the discordant chiming of the bells and the emptying of the Church in the first part, the character of Antonius appears in the second part as a guiding image in search of the 'inner' bell. This indicates a significant psychological reorientation, in which not only popular belief but also religious knowledge of our Christian culture seems to play an important role.

This brings us to the last important attribute of Saint Antonius, namely, the cross, the central Christian symbol. It also plays the main role in the second part of my dream, coming after the church has emptied. A large cross sinks down from above into the hand of Antonius. So apparently the situation is not simply a matter of walking out of the church and thus abandoning the Christian myth. On the contrary, it seems as though the central symbol of this myth must be 'grasped' and so understood in a new and different way, with a significant meaning distilled from it. This new way is the symbolic method of interpretation, which links the unconscious background of the psyche to conscious perceptions.

Fig. 35: Saint with cross. Workshop of the “Meister der großen Nasen”, 1505.

8. The Cross

In order to be able to examine more closely the symbolic background of the cross, we shall deal first with the traditional meanings handed down to us in popular and Christian traditions. The topic of the cross will summarise and reconnect us with the previous chapters.

In most illustrations of Antonius the Egyptian, he is usually shown with his most important attribute: a long staff with an 'Antonius cross'. It has the shape of a so-called *Tau* cross, also referred to as the Egyptian or Coptic cross. This cross was already found in pre-Christian times in Egypt and in the Orient, but then later it appeared on the staffs of the Antonite monks and on the Franciscan's too. Antonius can also sometimes be seen carrying a hand cross, either as a Tau cross or an isosceles one, a Greek cross or a Latin one, which has its vertical bar extended downwards. Such a cross appeared in the dream described earlier as initiating this work.

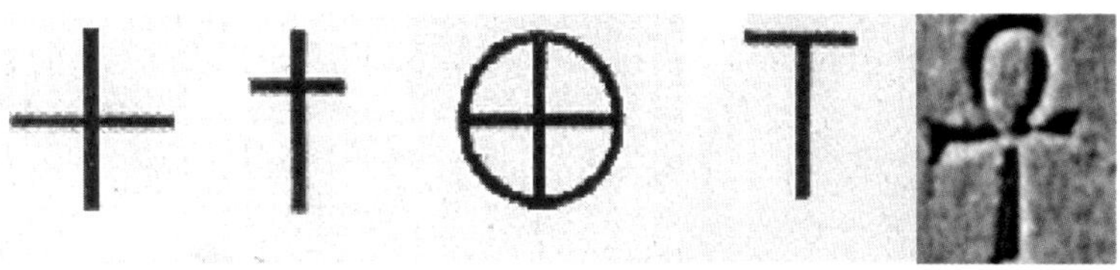

Fig. 36: Forms of Crosses. Greek Cross, Latin Cross, Wheel Cross. Tau or Antonius Cross, Ansate Cross.

The cross in various forms, such as the Tau cross, the swastika, or the wheel cross, can be found in the pre-Christian era and, as a significant magical and religious symbol, it even appears in cave drawings from the Stone Age. The original function of the cross probably lays in the dividing up of the 'Lebensraum' (the living space) into the four points of the compass, the four points of the horizon, as an aid to basic orientation. For archaic man, this meant orientation in the chaos of the cosmos, which was evidently such an amazing discovery that he was motivated to illustrate it in stone, an achievement that seems incredible to us today. This division of space into quarters can be identified even in the very first temples of humankind hitherto known to us, one example being Stone-Age *Göbekli Tepe* recently discovered in Anatolia.[122]

The enormous significance of creating order by division of the whole into quarters is that it demonstrates the very beginning of the development of human consciousness. Jung points out that this process is driven and supported by nature or instinct itself. There is an innate human urge to strive for higher and greater awareness. «One is hardly conscious of the extent to which nature acts not only as a driving-force but as a helper – in other words, how much instinct insists that the higher level of consciousness be attained. This urge to a higher and more comprehensive consciousness fosters civilisation and culture. [...].»[123] On a personal level, it allows the self – out of a confused mass of sensations, impressions or experiences – to establish a framework, an order. It can make us suddenly 'see the light' about how things are connected, which can pave the way for a state of calmness.

Thus the cross in this original meaning symbolized – in contrast to the archaic, chaotic state of being at the mercy of circumstances, moods and emotions – the emergence of a differentiated point of view. Psychologically this focal point, from which order can be established, is the self. This detached point of view and the aforementioned focal point, symbolised by the cross, is the self. It prevents consciousness from being sucked back into chaos. Archaic peoples sensed that there was something which had the numinous power to protect them from the original state of chaos, which is why all their initiation rites and mysteries revolved around this self.

Indeed the paramount importance of the cross in the Christian faith indicates that it can be viewed as a magical sign of protection and defence against the forces of darkness. In popular belief, the cross played a major role in warding off ghosts and demons. A cross is carried for this purpose by Antonius and also by many other saints. Psychological experience

122 See Th. Abt, "*Göbekli Tepe*: Kulturelles Gedächtnis und das Wissen der Natur". In: *Zeitschrift für Orient-Archäologie,* (ZOrA 7, 2014), p. 103.

123 See C.G. Jung, *The Practice of Psychotherapy* [CW 16], § 471.

shows that the cross often appears as a four-part mandala in states of mental disorder, these being mostly caused by the invasion of unconscious contents. In Jung's view, this was undoubtedly a common phenomenon in the early days of Christianity.[124]

Modern consciousness is not as far removed from the chaotic world of the original unconscious state as it might seem. Our protective walls of common sense are still thin and can cave in at any time. The demons can still pose a real threat to civilised consciousness, only nowadays they are given different names. What psychic forces are we dealing with here? And what is the role played by the cross as a symbol of the self in this drama?

In her book, *Projection and Re-collection in Jungian Psychology,* M.-L. von Franz speaks about the belief in demons among peoples in all ages from time immemorial.[125] She shows, by taking a closer look at the different notions of good and evil spirits in the ancient world, that one can understand these demonic forces as instinctual and emotional parts of the archetypes, that is, as psychic conditions. So archetypal psychic conditions appear in the world view of early man, projected as demons and spirits. Today, in psychological language, we call them autonomous complexes of the unconscious. This means that they belong essentially to our mental functioning.

We can therefore say with M.-L. von Franz, that the demons are «the archetypal formations that appear in the field of human projections.»[126] Indeed, we can only recognise an archetype if it somehow draws attention to itself in the outside world. The archetype of the mother can, for example, only be indirectly identified and described via its manifestation in the mother complex. Whenever in a dispute such a complex is touched, it immediately triggers off violent emotions which, in the case of the mother complex, go far beyond the responsibility of the personal mother and can completely disempower consciousness. Then self-control is abandoned. The demons are off the leash! At that moment, the archetypal background

124 C. G. Jung, "Transformation Symbolism in the Mass", in: *Psychology and Religion: West and East* [CW 11], § 432f.

125 M.-L. von Franz, *Projection and Re-collection,* p. 107f.

126 Ibid., p. 117.

of the problem cannot usually be seen, which is why someone else or a specific situation has to take the blame! Standard procedure in any dispute! Inner processes and conditions are instinctively projected onto the other, the enemy, the external circumstances.

The reason why projections are so demonic is that they distort reality, be it positively or negatively. If we look carefully, we can sometimes quite clearly see projections of internal processes in others in everyday life. The eternal troublemaker in the neighbourhood, who accuses everyone else of being quarrelsome, the man who feels that he has not been given his full due, who fights his unconscious claims to power in others, and so on. However it is much more difficult to come to terms with one's own projections, because the essence of the demons is precisely that they represent that in us which is unconscious, not 'known'.

In a certain sense, positive or negative projections establish a connection to our outside world, without us actually being aware of it. It seems that some people, especially if they live alone, can only establish relationships with other people by means of projections, often in the form of blasphemy and unpleasant chatter. The age we live in means that the solitary individual – no longer embedded in a family or village community, where everyone knew each other, including their shadow sides – has become more prone to projections than ever. For the more unfamiliar our surroundings and the people around us are, the easier it is for our own inner realities to be projected onto them. We actually only realise we are projecting when our own ideas clash with the reality of the outside world. Only then can we recognise them as projections. And yet we ask ourselves how it comes about that enlightened man, with a portion of self-criticism, still hardly recognises these unconscious, demonic forces before they can unleash their destructive effects? One reason may be connected with Western culture, and the historical development of Christian thought, something that Jung worked on in several of his works. We thus propose looking back in time to the first centuries of Christianity.

In his work *Psychological Types,* Jung speaks about the bishops of that era. As an example, he singles out Athanasius of Alexandria, the author of the *Vita Antonii* and he quotes from the exhortations of the bishop to the monks: «There is a time when we see no man and yet the sound of the working of the devils is heard by us, and it is like the singing of a song in a loud voice; and there are times when the words of the Scriptures are heard by us, just as if a living man were repeating them, and they are exactly like the words which we should hear if a man were reading the Book. And it also happens that they [the devils] rouse us up to the night prayer, and incite us to stand up; [...] (And they say:) "How is it possible for thee to live? For thou hast sinned and committed iniquity in many things. Thinkest thou, that the Spirit hath not revealed unto me what hath been done by thee, or that I know not that thou hast done such and such a thing?" [...] It is then (Anthanasius continues) unnecessary for us to be terrified at these things, and we have need to fear only when the devils multiply the speaking of the things *which are true* and then we must rebuke them severely [...]. Let us take heed that we incline not our hearing to their words, even though they be word of truth which they utter [...]. And let us, o my brethren, arm ourselves with the armour of righteousness, and let us put on the helmet of redemption, and in the time of contending let us shoot out from a believing mind spiritual arrows as from a bow which is stretched. For they (the devils) are nothing at all, and even if they were, their strength has in it nothing which would enable it to resist the might of the Cross.»[127]

According to Antonius, everything that has an effect on solitary prayer and fasting, on voices and visions, is simply an attempt by the demons and the Devil to bring about the downfall of those involved. Only Christ and the cross can make them disappear. The cross here is utterly and exclusively a means of fending off the demons. Even back then, the effect it had on people can be seen in the furious reaction of the Devil. According to Jung, the Devil is the voice of the hermit's own unconscious, which is incensed at the vicious repression of individual nature. In those days, by imposing the generally held beliefs, the bishops were trying to stamp out the effectiveness of the individual unconscious among the monks «despite the fact that it transparently spoke the truth.»[128]

Here we recall the legend, in which the Devil himself complained to Antonius that the Christians and monks cursed him. Antonius then asked him why he tormented them. The Devil's answer was:

127 C. G. Jung, *Psychological Types* [CW 6], § 82.

128 Ibid., § 83.

«I am not the one who troubles them, but they trouble themselves, because it happened to me, which is true, that they would have killed themselves, if I had not called to them that I was the enemy. I have become weak. I have no longer a place, a weapon, a city. The Christians are spread everywhere, and at length even the desert is filled with monks. Let them take heed to themselves, and let them not curse me undeservedly.»[129]

The Devil here presents the situation as though he had to offer himself as a scapegoat, because people would otherwise have killed themselves. We have already seen that at this time, in response to the uninhibited sensuality of late Antiquity, it was actually necessary for a while "to have a devil", that is, to be able to project evil externally, so that a light and bright side could be acknowledged and striven for. According to the legend, this was brought on by the Devil, in other words, by the unconscious itself. Even so, the Devil complained about his 'demonization'. The problem of repression is already visible, although it also meant that a significant step forward was in the offing, namely the awareness of good and evil, an ordering of the previous state of chaos. Part of this process, as we have seen, is achieved by the cross in its discriminating function.

However, the cross also subsequently became the symbol of the *Imitatio Christi*, thus completely depriving the Devil of his power: «I no longer have a place where I could be [...].» As Christianity gained ground, more and more demons (with the exception of some nature spirits) together with all earlier pagan deities, came to be regarded as evil. God, Christ, and certain angels, meanwhile, were seen in an entirely positive light. Athanasius says: «[...] for they (the devils) are nothing at all, and even if they were, their strength has nothing in it which would enable them to resist the might of the cross.»[130] This makes it clear that Satan is basically to be understood as something that does not actually exist. But as we have seen, according to the legend, the Devil definitely wants to be acknowledged.

According to M.-L. Franz, this demand on the part of the demons for public cultic honours appears also in other writings of the early church fathers, even in public cult ceremonies, and it was to play a role in exorcism

129 E. A. Wallis-Budge, *Vita Antonii,* (The Life of St. Antony).

130 C. G. Jung, *Psychological Types* [CW 6], § 82.

until the late 17th century.[131] In the exorcism of Sister Delphine of Stans in Switzerland in 1847, Lucifer expresses his abhorrence of sin and warns people about it! At the same time, he announces how people can best be tempted to sin, thus revealing his own working method as it were! He then predicts disaster for the country and advises people to make supplications to brother Niklaus von Flüe, and at other local shrines. These statements by the devil triggered off a veritable stream of pilgrimages to Sachseln and Stans and a bout of almost feverish religious activity. People, including some of the lesser clergy, took this advice from the Devil very seriously.[132] It was in fact the voice of the unconscious, which was saying things they regarded as true. However, this instinct-related behaviour contrasted sharply with the prevailing spiritual attitude of the Age of Enlightenment, which dismissed the existence of demons as mere illusion, so no reference to these unconscious powers was possible.

This Enlightenment attitude meant that the powers of darkness or evil, or the unknown aspects of the psyche in general, even though they continued to exist and still do, became so unreal for people that they no longer knew how to deal with them. While ghosts and demons were still a reality for early man, something he had to learn to live with and protect himself against, later there was nothing to remind enlightened man that ultimately he was only to a very limited extent master of his own house.

In the soaring flight of the enlightened spirit, to which we owe all our contemporary knowledge of science and technology, we have completely lost sight of the unconscious side, our shadow side, which is actually the source of our creative ideas, but also of their unpleasant and often inexplicable side effects. The invention of the automobile was undoubtedly a great thing. But in the Lötschen Valley, for example, when the new Post bus came along, conveniently linking the Valley with the outside world for the first time, people saw its black trailer and thought that the Devil was sitting inside it. In so doing, they were intuitively and correctly expressing the notion that a sinister demonic power follows hot on the heels of progress. At that time, the idea of environmental pollution and destruction of nature, with all its external and internal consequences,

131 M.-L. von Franz, *Projection and Re-Collection*, p. 114.

132 P. Hugger, *Schwester Delphine von Stans,* p. 152 and 154 f.

Fig. 37: Christ's *Descensus ad Inferos*. Bookpainting. Sinai, Cloister of St. Katharine.

had not crossed anybody's mind. But it is man who designed the first car, and it is man who now works in laboratories on the development of nuclear weapons and other dangerous inventions. With this one-sidedly rational approach, technical development releases unconscious demonic forces. As neither demons nor the relevant contents of the unconscious are a reality for modern consciousness, like physical organs that have been neglected, they become increasingly destructive. The polarisation of conscious and unconscious becomes ever more pronounced.

This psychic split relates to the one-sided development of the Christian God image in our culture. Any notion of God is an expression of a psychological fact. Thus the figure of Christ, as Jung has shown, represents a parallel to the phenomenon of the self. We shall try to shed more light on this psychological term, even if what the self represents in the psyche can only be expressed in images.

M.-L. Franz explains it as follows: The self manifests out of the unconscious as «a kind of midpoint or centre in which the supreme value and the greatest life-intensity are concentrated. It cannot be distinguished from the images of the supreme value of the various religions. It appears as naturally in the individuation process as it does in the religions, in the Christian world for example as an 'inner castle' (Teresa of Avila), a four-square city or garden, as the *scintilla animae*, as the *imago Dei* in the soul, as the "circle whose periphery is nowhere and whose centre is everywhere", as a crystal, a stone, a tree, a vessel or a cosmic order; or, again, as in Eastern religions, as a golden four-petalled flower, as light, as a 'void' filled with meaning. The experience of this highest end, or centre, brings the individual an inner certainty, peace and sense of meaning and fulfillment, in the presence of which he can accept himself and find a middle way between the opposites in his inner nature. Instead of being a fragmented person who has to cling to collective supports, he now becomes a self-reliant whole human being who no longer needs to live like a parasite off his collective environment, but who enriches it and strengthens it by his presence. The experience of the self brings a feeling of standing on solid ground inside oneself, on a patch of inner eternity which even physical death cannot touch.»[133]

This self, as a kind of concept of wholeness or a vision of the individuation process is structured as a possibility in the psyche of every human being, but it is not infallibly implemented in the natural, organic life process of the individual. «For it does not depend so very greatly on knowledge and ability or upon some degree of intelligence, but rather upon the use which is made of these attributes and above all, on the psychic attitude a person adopts in the face of the various circumstances of his life and fate. As the threads of fabric are woven into a pattern, so the self as the living garment of divinity is woven out of the many decisions and crises, in themselves possibly insignificant, by which we are affected in the course of our lives. Such occasions present themselves at every level of life and intelligence and in every milieu. Whether or not they lead to a manifestation of the self depends solely on our own response.»[134]

The spontaneous symbols of the self, or of wholeness, as they appear also in dreams, fantasies and visions, cannot in practice be distinguished

133 M.-L. von Franz, *C. G. Jung. His Myth in our Time*, p. 73f.

134 E. Jung and M.-L. von Franz, *The Grail Legend,* p. 134.

from a god-image.[135] But Jung explains that «In the empirical self [that is in practical, human experience - author's note] light and shadow form a paradoxical unity. In the Christian concept, on the other hand, the archetype is helplessly split into two irreconcilable halves, leading ultimately to a metaphysical dualism – the final separation of the kingdom of heaven from the fiery world of the damned.»[136]

The development and differentiation of Christian consciousness, which has separated evil from the god-image and made Christ representative of only good, has led inevitably to a conflict, an irreconcilable opposition. For in the creation of a good God, there should actually be no Devil. Following this line of reasoning, Christian theologians, with their idea of *privation boni*, tried to explain him away, defining evil as "a mere diminution of good". Certain Protestant sects subsequently eliminated the Devil entirely from their theology.[137] These developments have had a major influence on the way we now deal with the unconscious.

Although in the Christian tradition, Jesus was an ordinary man, and certainly has normal human traits in the Bible, Christ nevertheless represented an image of perfection. This image of Christ comes from an innate striving for perfection which, as Jung says, represents one of the most powerful roots of cultural growth and development.[138] According to Jung, however, psychological experience shows that the archetype of the self strives for completeness, rather than for perfection. Aspiring to completeness as a goal is more human and more realistic, because it does not mean just being good, but also includes the less good and even evil. If the perfect figure of Christ has now become a symbol of the self, this is a paradox, since striving for perfection is bound to be thwarted by the tendency of the archetype to fulfill itself in completeness. In other words, where there is too much conscious striving towards perfection, the self enforces completeness. The demons, which demand attention and which speak the truth, are part of this completeness. Thus the more uncompromisingly Antonius behaves in the desert in his rejection of the temptation to sin, the

135 C. G. Jung, *Aion* [CW 9/II], § 73.

136 Ibid., § 76.

137 Ibid., § 74.

138 This and the following see C. G. Jung, *Aion* [CW 9/II], § 123f.

more unruly the behaviour of the demons. The 'discipleship of God' or, in other words, the realisation of the self leads therefore to a fundamental conflict. «The individual may strive after perfection [...] but must suffer from the opposite of his intentions for the sake of his completeness.»[139] This condition amounts to a painful realisation of the fact that the balance of consciousness, despite every effort, can be upset and threatened at any time by chaotic contents of the unconscious.

As we have seen, where there is confusion arising from restlessness or disorientation, quaternity symbols, such as the cross, which since time immemorial have expressed the deepest meaning in various religions, bring resolution through the compensating principle of order. The cross therefore depicts not only the suffering of crucifixion between the opposites, but also the union of warring opposites. It eases the way to a healthier and quieter state, a 'salvation'.[140] In this sense, the cross of Saint Antonius, who has become the patron saint of domesticated animals, can be understood not so much as offering protection against demons and devils, but rather as a means of giving them due consideration or of listening to them. It becomes then the expression of a new psychological attitude, which refers the demons back to where they come from, namely within the inner reality. Part of the destructive demonry is thus removed from the outside world, where it turns out to be a shadow projection. Taking the inner demons seriously would be the 'religious ceremony' which they demand, a conscious acknowledgement of the inner spiritual forces of darkness and an acceptance of the ensuing conflict and suffering.

If we enter into discussion with the demons on our inner stage, in other words, with the unconscious players in our life dramas, we can find ourselves on unfamiliar moral ground. Dreams can bring up figures who are morally ambivalent and if we wish to take them seriously, as part of ourselves, good and evil may suddenly become less clearly defined. For if we are prepared to concede that even a demon may speak the truth, the walls that structure our Christian thinking and neatly separate good from evil, start to crumble and anything seems possible. We can no longer rely on generally valid guidelines for judging what is good and what is bad, for

139 Ibid., § 123.

140 Ibid., § 304.

determining how much evil is part of our own nature, or to what extent we may condone something outside the boundaries of what is usually acceptable. For example, we may have consciously condemned our own 'sinful' behaviour, but then a dream shows it in less black and white terms, or even as necessary from the instinctual or unconscious point of view. Or, if we have been kidding ourselves that we have behaved correctly, the unconscious may throw a spanner in the works with a dream that poses uncomfortable questions. Am I – or am I not – doing a fellow human being a good turn with my loving attention? Is there a real relationship here or is there not a good deal of selfishness and egotism behind it all? Or does the other person need something quite different from loving attention at the moment? Where are the limits and how far is it our personal responsibility to interfere in the unconscious world of darkness? We find ourselves in the middle of a conflict, crucified between opposing forces within ourselves, or, at "war against one's own heart", as it says in the legend.

When in the middle of a crowd pushing and shoving, Antonius says that he was accustomed to a much larger crowd of demons in the desert, it seems as if a kind of living together with them had finally become viable for him, after the tremendous torment he had endured. In accordance with our Christian myth, confrontation with the demonic sides of human nature entails conscious suffering. That means no longer shirking responsibility for the shadow, no longer behaving like Crusaders and witch-hunters seeing wickedness only in others, no longer feeling entitled to enlighten one's neighbour, or in ideological blindness setting out to improve the world. Whenever the good that we want to do feels so compelling that we are driven by it, we must be prepared for the fact that somewhere evil will consolidate its position. Then, not only within us psychologically, but also in the outside world, the tension between the opposites is exacerbated.

If, later on, we find Antonius depicted with a cross in his hand, we could say that, as well as having demonstrated the conscious struggle with the demons, he now becomes the model of a personality able to tolerate and reconcile the contradictions ripped apart by Christian thinkers. He was able to recognise the dark side of God, later known as the *Deus absconditus,* and to stand firm against it. The concept of *Deus absconditus* comes from Luther. Amazingly, he made the distinction between the God of love, of whom the Bible speaks, calling him the *Deus manifestus,* and the dark side of the same God, the *Deus absconditus*, the hidden God. This dark is seen in the violent-tempered, vengeful God of the Old Testament, who, inexplicably, betrayed his pious servant Job to the Devil.[141] In the *Deus absconditus*, the Devil is, so to speak, connected to the divine, the split between heaven and hell is the problem of the one God. In the symbol of the cross, these two sides of God meet in conflict and are at the same time united and reconciled.

The pig, the fire and the bell seem to some extent to bridge the irreconcilable opposites of good and evil or saint and devil, for they belong to our daily lives and have their function there, while also symbolising unconscious archetypal realities. Put simply, the pig has to do with the sphere of physical drives, while the fire relates to the energy, the libido which "fires the processes of life". The bell, as we have seen, is a symbol of the *vox Dei*, expressing both bright and dark aspects of God. All three symbols provide a connection between the conscious and the unconscious worlds, a bridge over the abyss of hell, which over the centuries, was torn open by the one-sidedness of the Christian Church. Like the archetypes behind them, they have both positive and negative impacts on our everyday life. Popular sentiment has thus in a very natural way made the ascetic saint human! With the cross, a symbol of the self, which combines in its centre the opposites of good and evil, above and below, left and right, a possibility of their being integrated on the level of consciousness is indicated.

The image of Antonius with the cross could be hinting at a possible psychological development which does not exclude the dark side of the unconscious and yet does not fall victim to it. It could point to the birth of a new attitude or perspective, a 'divine child', uniting opposites, like the black child that Antonius encountered in his vision. It could point to the birth of a new god-image embracing both light and dark aspects of the divinity. But in order to accept and endure the dark God, the *Deus absconditus*, without being destroyed, we will require, as Jung says, more light, kindness and moral force, in other words, more of the Christian virtues, as well as wisdom. When one is dealing with darkness, with the shadow, «one must cling to the good, otherwise one will be devoured

141 C. G. Jung, *Visions. Notes of the Seminar, given in 1930-1934,* p. 845.

by the devil.»[142] Thus our personal sense of responsibility must remain imbued with the Christian ethos, because if we cast it off, we – with our 2000 years of Christian past – are totally at the mercy of an evil that knows no bounds. The Christian myth, as Jung repeatedly emphasised, still serves a purpose in this day and age. Were this not the case, essential further development would not be possible, namely the addition of the dark side of God to his bright image and its rebirth in man. The God of love, whom we may dismiss as a sentimental and antiquated white-bearded old man on his throne in heaven, needs a new face, but we can only wait for it to emerge, in an unexpected way, from the depths of the unconscious psyche.

But this birth in man, like the birth of Christ, occurs in a place that is despised: in a manger, alongside ox and donkey, close to animal nature. Usually it takes a major effort for us to turn seriously to the images and instinctive impulses that arise from our inner world. They are initially difficult to understand and we may dismiss them as meaningless and worthless. It may be even more difficult to bring what they call for consciously into life, and our efforts in this direction rarely lead to swift or dramatic changes. Indeed, it is wise first to venture into this invisible area with small and unspectacular steps. Living as we are today in a predominantly outward-oriented, fast-moving age, it is incredibly difficult to view these tentative inward steps as meaningful. There is a connection here with the devil, the bell, the pig and the fire. They all lead initially into the unknown, into things we were not previously aware of and did not think possible. But because only an experience of this nature can lead to something more than just a temporary change of attitude, the psychology of the unconscious is beyond most people's comprehension. People are usually convinced that they already know all that they need to know about themselves, despite the fact that in reality their own powerlessness repeatedly forces them to their knees.

Let us take the example of the bell. We have understood it as an inner voice which is able to connect the conscious field of everyday life with its unconscious background. Listening to the bell can mean acknowledging a basic context for our own internal processes or attributes in external

142 C. G. Jung, "Answer to Job". In: *Psychology and Religion: West and East* [CW 11], § 742.

occurrences, which then become meaningful in a new way. A person who really gets on my nerves, for example, usually does so because, if I am honest, I can also detect some of his attributes in myself. Accidents often happen when we are particularly at odds with ourselves, so that we are actually tripped up by our own unconscious. Similarly, in a dispute, an opponent's attack may hit our most sensitive weak spot precisely because our own lack of insight means that we are unable to protect ourselves. Connecting an external incident, such as a dispute, to those aspects of our own character that get us into trouble can be a very unpleasant experience, but if we succeed, it actually takes some of the steam out of the external incident. If this happens, the outer confrontation does not necessarily become unimportant, but intolerance and complacency that have fuelled it tend to fade away and then a solution may begin to emerge. That is why taking an honest look inside of ourselves in such a situation has nothing to do with selfish 'contemplation of the navel'. On the contrary, it brings about a deeper understanding of external incidents and a more genuine relationship to them than can be achieved by focussing merely on our good intentions.

Jung illustrates the way this psychological reality plays out on a collective level in the relationship between nations. He says that a direct democracy wages fewer wars abroad than a totalitarian state, because in a democracy people are preoccupied with internal warfare, that is, with the constant confrontations of opposing political parties and interest groups. This means that, relatively speaking, the chances of peace with foreign countries are greater. However, the chances of lasting peace would be greater still if the next step were also taken, which would mean individuals taking 'war' into themselves.[143] This inner war is the personal confrontation with the shadow, with all the demons that we otherwise fight through our projections onto the outside world. The internal warfare would take up so much energy and make such demands on our resources that fighting with our neighbours would simply not enter into the equation of life. Yet we do our utmost to avoid the inner war because it means that we are left completely to our own devices, with nobody else to blame and nobody to

143 See C. G. Jung, "The Fight with the Shadow". In: *Civilisation in Transition* [CW 10], § 444-457.

ease the suffering that war involves. Defeat, whichever side it falls to in the inner battle, is always our problem. On the other hand, it is relatively easy to fight evil in the outer enemy, because then we feel we are firmly on the good side. As history has shown, declaring war on a neighbouring country has often been a strategy for preserving unity in one's own country.

Fighting for good and against evil – in itself a legitimate desire – corresponds to our longing for perfection. Despite the widespread mood of pessimism that prevails today, people still somehow have the idea that if you get things just right, and are good, sensible and idealistic enough, then the world will ultimately be in order. We cling to this notion with all our might. It includes thinking we know what needs to be done, what would be good or not good, even though at every turn we meet people who have different ideas, probably not without justification. It is unlikely that anybody entirely escapes the temptation to presume time and again to know what is good and what is bad. We all have certain notions of right and wrong, certain moral values, which we feel – with no trace of arrogance – that we have to abide by. However, where any claim to perfection is involved, be it for ourselves, or for our external world, the dangers of hypocrisy and fanaticism arise and all too easily open the backdoor for the very evil we are fighting with the best of intentions. But wherever people can succeed in acknowledging their own dark side, their dishonest intentions, thirst for power, self-importance, bad moods, anger, aggression, selfishness, sexual compulsions, and so on, without becoming overwhelmed by them, then a step towards completeness replaces the striving for the never-to-be-achieved goal of perfection. At the same time, it is worth recalling again that Jung makes it very clear, that choosing the path of completeness requires every single ounce of our potential of goodness, since otherwise the scales will inevitably tip onto the side of evil.

The idea of salvation, which is inextricably linked to the cross, is perhaps, in part, associated with a 'redeeming' insight that finally allows me to do the right thing, after taking into account the conflicting points of view. There are no general guidelines for this 'right thing', so I can never know it in advance; either it appears, or often it does not. Salvation is ultimately not up to me alone and it involves 'crucifixion'. This means that despite the greatest possible ethical effort, there is no avoiding the fact that I may be constantly thwarted by the workings of inner and outer circumstances. Even the fact that I may do the wrong thing, is, in the final analysis, part of my cross and has to do with completion.[144]

On the subject of completeness, the question arises as to what sort of relationship Saint Antonius, being a man and an ascetic, had to the feminine. There is no way of knowing for certain. We have, however, seen that his attributes, as they have evolved in our Western culture, contain in symbolic form certain feminine values. His connections with the sphere of instinct, with the emotional and feeling dimensions of life, and with the inner, psychological perspective all show an appreciation of values that were suppressed by the official Christian teaching with its emphasis on the quest for perfection. This striving for perfection, however little we realise it, is still at the base of much contemporary thinking. The pervasive idea that only the latest and most modern is the best, and that we are apparently on the road to even better things, is a prime example. As we have already hinted in the Pig and Bell chapters, the consequences of such a one-sided collective attitude for women today are more far-reaching than they are for men.

Jung says that for women, who by nature are more inclined to strive for completeness, there is a special danger lurking behind the male claim to perfection. This explains why the many campaigns for equal rights for men and women are not without problems.[145] In striving too much for perfection, a woman becomes unfaithful to her own nature, because she either forgets or underestimates the notion of completeness. A man's nature, on the other hand, can, as Jung ironically puts it, sustain relative perfection better and for a longer period of time! In our Christian culture, the emphasis placed on the purity and virginity of Mary has made her a

144 C. G. Jung, "The Psychology of the Transference". In: *The Practice of Psychotherapy* [CW 16], § 470. «The Christian symbol of the crucifix is therefore a prototype and an 'eternal' truth. There are medieval pictures showing how Christ is nailed to the Cross by his own virtues. Other people meet the same fate at the hands of their vices. Nobody who finds himself on the road to wholeness can escape that characteristic suspension which is the meaning of crucifixion. For he will infallibly run into things that thwart and "cross" him: first, the thing he has no wish to be (the shadow); second, the thing he is not (the 'other', the individual reality of the 'You'); and third, his psychic non-ego (the collective unconscious).»

145 C. G. Jung, "Answer to Job". In: *Psychology and Religion: West and East* [CW 11], § 620.

model of feminine perfection, which has meant a violation of the feminine principle of completeness.[146]

Embracing the dark, hidden areas of life, in the way necessary for feminine completeness, is closely connected with the natural instincts, as we have seen in relation to the pig symbol. But for the woman today, because much of what belongs to our animal nature is difficult to bring in line with the ideal of perfection, it soon becomes the victim of male views and rational values. In the psyche of the individual woman, it is attacked by the animus. This animus voice argues in the spirit of the current Zeitgeist, which seeks to obliterate the boundaries and differences between men and women for ideological reasons and encourages the woman to sacrifice her own individuality to a general egalitarianism. Just how strongly her female instinct may try to defend itself can often be seen in dreams, in which animals are harmed, tortured or neglected, or else become aggressive and dangerous.[147]

Drawing to a conclusion our discussion of all the symbolism associated with the figure of Antonius, we can say that it is summed up in the symbol of the cross. The solitude in the desert, the battle with devils and demons, the transformation by and in the fire, the connection to the pig, the link between this world and the hereafter via the bell, all ultimately convey aspects of the Way of the Cross, as depicted in the Christian myth. At the same time, from a psychological point of view, they depict various stages and struggles encountered on the path of individuation. The promise of salvation implicit in the cross can be understood as meaning there is something in man that helps him to venture along this difficult path, to acknowledge and accept the opposites, to trust in his own destiny, and to become 'more complete'. Not perfect, just more complete. Animals are not perfect either, but by nature they fully abide by the divine will – they are what they were made to be – whereas man suffers from irrevocably being cut off from nature. But it seems that going back into nature, in the sense of returning to a state of animal unconsciousness, is not an option, for Nature – or God himself – both forces us and at the same time helps us towards conscious awareness. Jesus did not do take this step for us. Those

146 Ibid., § 620.

147 See R. Abt-Baechi, *Animals and Animal Dreams.*

who are 'meant' have to take it for themselves, as did Antonius the hermit, the loner. Adapting a phrase from M.-L. von Franz, we can say that, in this sense, the *imitatio Christi* of Antonius is exemplary, in the courageous way he acknowledged and struggled with the opposites and in his faithfulness to his inner experience of God.[148]

148 See M.-L. von Franz, unpublished part of an interview with S. Wagner.

Final Word

Returning to the dream that began this work, I ask myself what it has to say about my personal situation then and now. And, more generally, in a period of inner and outer uncertainty and doubt, what does it have to contribute to the traditional, ecclesiastical image of God? As the daughter of a Catholic mother and Protestant father, who both described themselves as non-religious, I had grown up with nothing I could draw on to explain the painful experiences of my past, nor the menacing darkness I saw in the world outside. Where was the kind, almighty God I had heard about in Sunday School, the God who allegedly loved us, yet whom we constantly had to beseech to deliver us from evil? Then the dream confronted me with the image of a saint, familiar to me only by his unusual relationship to the pig. Realising that there had to be more to this figure, and that it clearly had to do with the religious question and my uncertain foothold in the world, I set out to discover what I could about him that might help me to understand the dream. This book is the outcome of that quest. Through it, I realised finally that the dream gives me no direct answer to the question of the dying Christian image of God and the evil in the world, but it turns my attention elsewhere.

Antonius took up the battle with the demons in the solitude of the desert, thus denying himself of the possibility of holding his fellow men or his outer circumstances responsible for the dark side of his own psyche. "Those who sit and repose in isolation have three battles fewer to fight: they can no longer be misled by seeing, hearing and speaking. There is just one battle left to face: against the heart". For the hermit, however, the demons were so tangible that they tortured him to the point of unconsciousness. In modern terms, that means that he was overwhelmed by the repressed, dark contents of the unconscious. The more passionately he strove for holiness, the more furiously the demons plagued him. However, the legends about his life that have been handed down to us, reveal a tendency towards a more conscious way of dealing with the forces of evil. In the course of

Fig. 38: “Niche of the precious cross”, Cloister of St. Anthony on the Red Sea.

the centuries, the original image of the hermit of extreme asceticism, portrayed in early traditional Christian iconography, was complemented by other, more human and more differentiated portraits of Antonius. Thus he became a popular saint, uniting the conflicting human qualities that we can all experience. The devils, the pig, the bell and the fire, as psychic forces, are all capable of destroying a person but also of elevating him, depending on how he responds to them. With the passage of time, Antonius became the role model of a personality who courageously faces up to the inner psychic powers and, overcoming all difficulties, finds a right and proper way of dealing with them. This is why in his pictures we also see his friendly connection to the pig and to certain aspects of the feminine.

In this way, the image of Antonius above and beyond his actual life has survived and developed through centuries of tradition. He has become, so to speak, a part of the human psyche, and thus a part of myself. If he appears in my dream, my personal question connects with the question of the many and my personal destiny connects to the destiny of the many. However, if he is a role model, who is able to bring together the incomprehensible contradictions in human and divine nature, then he can ultimately only do so in my own soul. There, and apparently nowhere else, Antonius has something to say to a modern person such as myself. But how is one to understand that?

At the centre of the dream is the cross, which is supposed to come down into the hand of Antonius. Oddly enough it initially hangs above him, then it comes down too far, before it is finally lifted up into his hand by solar warmth. Too high above must be understood as too intellectual, too spiritual, too remote from everyday life and understanding. With the passage of time, what the symbolism of the cross has come to mean for me and for many has probably become 'too high', too abstract, too unnatural and thus meaningless. As a result, the cross has dropped too far down, into the emptiness of a materialistic worldview, which leaves the most burning questions of life unanswered. (This situation is also represented by the part of the dream where the church has emptied and the bells are clashing discordantly.) Through the sun's warmth, however, the cross can now come into the hands of Antonius. According to the dream, he is apparently only an image initially, but then becomes a living figure, who can grasp the cross. Something seems to have come to life in the psyche, which before had been only a suspended image, a lifeless picture that had no meaning for me.

The cross is a symbol of the union of the psychic opposites represented in the figure of Antonius. As we have learned from Jung, it represents not merely a symbol of the self but also the goal of individuation, a person's attainment of wholeness. Thus the cross, which is supposed to deliver us from all suffering and yet apparently fails to do so, in fact points to an individual task that has now moved into the inner psychic realm. Antonius, in accordance with his traditional role as a saint, makes this task possible and offers a helping hand. In a simple way, he embodies a spirit associated with life, with the hardships and temptations experienced by ordinary people. Viewing him in this way, the dream offers the possibility of a new religious concept that has little to do with the traditional church image of God, but almost exclusively with the reality of the psyche. This, apparently, is where 'salvation' is to be found; in other words, where a reconciliation of the opposites in one's own nature becomes possible. God, however, is not lost. Indeed, he is found closer to us, in the reality of our own experience.

In the dream, Antonius and the Cross are separated and are apparently meant to come together again. Initially the saint is merely a lifeless image with no particular function, a lifeless tradition, we could say, without meaning or effect. But then he seems to come alive, to be revived as a spiritual aspect of the psyche. This is brought about by the warmth of the sun, not the burning sun of the desert, but by the gentle sunlight which 'lifts up', as it was described in Antiquity. People at that time «were puzzled at the fact that the sun raised the water by warming it, so that clouds were formed, and that when the sun disappeared the rain would come, so the sun was often spoken of as the principle of spiritual elevation. It is that which makes things perfect; it exalts them to the heights and makes them visible.»[149]

The sun in this dream therefore has something to do with the "light of consciousness" which is able to raise the problem of the opposites in human and divine nature – a problem opened up by Christianity – onto a higher level, bringing it up from its bleak and dangerous immersion in

149 M.-L. von Franz, *Alchemy,* p. 150.

meaningless materialism to where it can be 'taken up' by the living spirit. If this were a burning sun, it would imply hostile passion, fanaticism, and new ideologies, associated with the familiar, age-old, projections of evil onto outer 'enemies'. The less intense and fiery warmth of the sun, however, has to do with loving care and attention, which accompanies and sustains the process of becoming conscious.

In the *Visions Seminar*, Jung explains that carrying a symbol or a god in a religious ritual always symbolises a transition from one state to another. It represented, for example, an essential aspect of the ancient mystery cults. Such a transition is also depicted in myths and heroic legends and is always connected with a painful or heroic act. In the Christian myth, too, Christ carries the cross along the road to his crucifixion.[150] So if my dream is emphasising the fact that Antonius is the living bearer of the cross, it is probably saying something about a difficult transition to a new 'understanding' and revitalisation of the central Christian symbol. This new understanding is not a theological but a psychological one, because it comes about in the dream in the house of M.-L. von Franz. On the level of the psyche, the traditional Christian saint can become a vital, natural spirit of renewal, able to grasp – and to unite – the painful contradictions of life, both conscious and unconscious. Antonius with his cross also represents the individual spiritual life, that has to stand against the superior strength of everything collective, be it the general rules, norms and attitudes of society, or the archetypal forces of the collective unconscious.

With the image of the Saint and the Cross, the dream has led me to examine more closely my rather naive Christian view of good and evil and my corresponding despair about the reality of the world. My preoccupation with Antonius and the pig thus became deeply meaningful for me.

As M.-L. von Franz points out in the preface to this book, this archetypal dream could also be understood in the context of a collective process, which is a given in the collective psyche, either as a possibility or necessity. The Christian figure of St. Antonius has been complemented by the unconscious formation of the legends and attributes attached to him making him a reconciling symbol of totality. In this way, he comes close the dual nature of the medieval Merlin or the alchemical Mercurius,

150 C. G. Jung, *Vision Seminars II,* p. 1211.

which combines good and evil, Christ and Antichrist within itself. Like Merlin or Mercurius, Antonius seems to embody a tendency to reunite the psychological opposites torn apart in the Christian teaching and so to heal the split in our collective psyche.[151] If such a symbolic figure appears in the dreams or creative fantasies of modern people, we know that this healing process continues and can manifest at any time in the individual.[152]

151 M.-L. von Franz, "Antichrist or Merlin?". In: *Archetypal Dimensions of the Psyche*, p. 29f.

152 It was only after I had completed this work that in the Red Book I happened to come across a lengthy example of active imagination involving an anchorite. It deals with the whole problem of opposites, which we also saw with Antonius. In the desert, Jung meets an Egyptian hermit by the name of Ammonius. This same Ammonius actually existed in the 3rd century, near the city of Alexandria. In the active imagination, Ammonius leaves the desert after the encounter with Jung in order to be among people, because Jung had told him that he probably needed to have people around him in order to gain access to the great mysteries. In this situation, he succumbs to the pleasures of wine and women and meets the devil, who prevents him from completely becoming a pig, and who is henceforth to become his travelling companion. In the active imagination the devil, the red rider, had also undergone a painful transformation after meeting Jung, with the result that he now needs the presence of the old hermit. The two wanderers, who are so dissimilar, do not like each other, but somewhat reluctantly acknowledge the other's right to exist. (The monk: "What is to be done? Even the devil is necessary, otherwise there is nothing with which to instil respect into people". And the devil: "The simple fact is that I have to form a pact with the clergy, otherwise I will lose my clientele.") The extreme opposites, the saint and the devil, good and evil, have come closer in this deep active imagination, which I can only hint at here.

Fig. 39: Cross pendant. Cloister of St. Anthony on the Red Sea.

Appendix

1. Bibliography

Abt-Baechi, Regina:

- *Animals and Animal Dreams,* Zurich 2011.
- *Princess and Magic Horse*, Zurich 2013.

Abt, Theodor:

- *Dark Clouds over Europe. Latent danger of renewed tyranny*, Zurich 2015.
- "*Göbekli Tepe*. Kulturelles Gedächtnis und das Wissen der Natur". In: *Zeitschrift für Orient-Archäologie* (ZOrA 7, 90–124), Berlin 2014.
- *Mushaf as-suwar. The Book of Pictures,* CALA II,1. Zurich 2007.
- *Progress without Loss of Soul,* Wilmette, Illinois 1989.

Aurenhammer, Hans: *Lexikon der christlichen Ikonographie*, vol. 1, Wien 1959-1967.

Athanasius: *Vita Antonii (VA),* Ed. Adolf Gottfried, Leipzig 1986.

Athanasius, Bishop of Alexandria: *Life of St. Anthony.* In: E.A. Wallis Budge, *The Book of Paradise. By Palladius, Hieronymus etc.* London 1904.

Bächtold-Stäubli, Hanns: *Handwörterbuch des deutschen Aberglaubens*, vol. II and vol. III, Berlin and Leipzig 1935/1936.

Von Beit Hedwig/M.-L. von Franz: *Symbolik des Märchens*, Bern/Munich 1971.

Benz, Richard (Ed.): *Legenda Aurea*, Heidelberg 1975.

Birkhäuser-Oeri, Sibylle: *The Mother - Archetypal Image in Fairy Tales, Toronto 1988.*

Bolman, Elisabeth S. (Editor) and Godeau, Patrick: *Monastic Visions. Wall Paintings in the Monastery of St. Antony on the Red Sea,* London 2002.

Büchli, Arnold: *Mythologische Landeskunde von Graubünden,* Disentis 1989-1990.

Butler, Dom Cuthbert: *The Lausiac History of Palladius,* Cambridge 1898/1904.

Brumagne, Marie-Magdaleine (Ed.): *Die Reise der Seele. Die Lebensgeschichte der Marie Métrailler.* Verlag Benziger 1991.

Devilliers, Noelle: *Antoine le Grand, Père des Moines*, Abbaye de Bellefontaine 1971.

von Franz, Marie-Louise:

- *Alchemy: An Introduction to the Symbolism and the Psychology.* Toronto 1982.
- *Archetypal Dimensions of the Soul*, London 1999.
- *Aurora Consurgens,* in: Jung, *Ges. Werke 14 III, Zurich 1957. (First Edition, not translated into English).*
- *C. G. Jung. His Myth in our Time*, Toronto 1998.
- *The Feminine in Fairytales*, Boston & London 1993.
- *The Golden Ass, New York 1970.*
- *The Passion of Perpetua, Dallas 1980. (German original: "Passio Perpetuae". In: C.G. Jung, Aion, Olten 1951).*
- "The Process of Individuation", in: C. G. Jung, *Man and his Symbols,* London 1979.
- *Projection and Re-Collection in Jungian Psychology*, Chicago 1995.
- *Unpublished excerpts from an Interview with S. Wagner.*

Von Franz, Marie-Louise /Jung, Emma: *The Grail Legend.* Princeton 1998.

Frazer, James George: *The Golden Bow: A Study in Magic and Religion.* London 1926.

Fried, J.: *Das Mittelalter. Geschichte und Kultur*. Munich 2009.

Gottfried, Adolf (Ed.): *Athanasius*: *Vita Antonii.* Leipzig 1986.

Graesse, Theodor (Ed.): *Jacobi a Voragine*: *Legenda Aurea*, Osnabrück, 1969.

Guntern, Josef: *Walliser Sagen,* Olten 1963.

Von Hertling, Ludwig: *Antonius der Einsiedler*, Innsbruck 1929.

Hoffmann-Krayer, Eduard: *Feste und Bräuche des Schweizervolkes*, Zurich 1913.

Hugger, Paul: *Schwester Delphine von Stans*. Zur Sinndeutung von Besessenheit und anderer paranormaler religiöser Phänomene aus einer besonderen geschichtlichen Situation. Separatum aus «Beiträge zur Geschichte Nidwaldens», 1980.

Huizinga, Johan: *Herbst des Mittelalters*, Munich 1928.

Hieronymus: *Vita Pauli* – The Latin Library, edited and translated by Hunink, Vincent. Leuven 2002.

Isler, Gotthilf:

- *Lumen Naturae,* Küsnacht 2000.
- *Die Sennenpuppe. Zur religiösen Funktion der Alpensagen*, Basle 1971.

Jung, Carl Gustav: [CW] = Collected Works

- *Aion* [CW 9/II], Princeton 1951.
- *The Archetypes and the Collective Unconscious* [CW 9/I], New York 1959.
- *Civilisation in Transition* [CW 10], New York 1970.
- *Letters*, vol. 1 and 2, Princeton 1984.
- *Memories, Dreams, Reflections,* New York 1989.
- *The Praxis of Psychotherapy* [CW 16], New York 1966.
- *Psychological Types* [CW 6], Princeton 1921.
- *Psychology and Alchemy* [CW 12], New York 1968.
- *Psychology and Religion, West and East* [CW 11], New York 1969.
- "A Psychological view of Conscience", in: *Civilisation in Transition* [CW 10], chapter 16. Translation from "das Gewissen in symbolischer Sicht" (symbolic view of conscience) in: *Das Gewissen*. Studien am C. G. Jung-Institut, vol. 7, Zurich 1958.
- *The Structure and Dynamics of the Psyche* [CW 8], New York 1969.
- *Symbols of Transformation* [CW 5], New York 1967.
- *Visions*. Notes from the Seminar given from 1930 – 1934. New Jersey 1997.

Jung, Emma/von Franz, Marie-Louise: *The Grail Legend.* Princeton 1998.

Korte, Gandulf: *Antonius der Einsiedler in Kult, Kunst und Brauchtum Westfalens,* Werl 1952.

Krutch, Josef W.: *The World of Animals. An Anthology of Lore, Legend, and Literature*, New Brunswick USA 2011.

Monick, Eugene: *An Archetypal Study of Grunewalds Isenheim Crucifixion*, Diploma Thesis C. G. Jung-Institut, Zurich 1977.

Müller, Josef: *Sagen aus Uri*, Basle 1969.

Nigg, Walter: *Das Geheimnis der Mönche,* Zurich 1953.

Reallexikon zur deutschen Kunstgeschichte, vol. 1, Stuttgart, 1937.

Patzel, Nikola: *Symbole im Landbau. Zur spirituellen Naturbeziehung in der Schweizer Agrarkultur.* Munich 2015.

Renner, Eduard: *Goldener Ring über Uri,* Zurich 1941.

Saint Antoinette: *Lettres*, Spiritualité Orientale, no 19, Abbaye de Bellefontaine 1976.

Sartori, Paul: *Das Buch von deutschen Glocken*, Berlin and Leipzig 1932.

Ström, Åke V., Harald Biezais: *Germanische und Baltische Religion*. Die Religionen der Menschheit; vol. 19,1, Stuttgart 1975.

Voragine, Jacobus de: *Die Legenda Aurea des Jacobus de Voragine*, Aus dem Lateinischen übersetzt von Richard Benz, Heidelberg 1975.

Wallis-Budge, E.A. (Ed.):

- *The Book of Paradise, by Palladius, Hieronimus, etc.* London 1904.
- *St. Athanasius: The Life of Saint Anthony*, Maryland 1950.

Weber-Kellermann, Ingeborg: *Deutsche Volkskunde zwischen Germanistik und Sozialwissenschaften*, Stuttgart 1969.

Zuckmayer, Carl: *Als wär's ein Stück von mir,* Wien 1966.

2. List of Illustrations

Chapter 5: The Fire

Chapter 6: The Pig

Chapter 7: The Bell

Chapter 8: The Cross

3. Index

– A –

– B –